An Unholy Mess

An Unholy Mess

Richard J. Dobbyn III

Contents

INTRODUCTION

Whenever I mentioned to friends or acquaintances that I was writing a memoir, they would politely say, "I would love to read it," or "That's nice; good for you." Since I am long retired and in my seventies, I believe people think I wanted to create a history for the family, or that it is a therapeutic exercise to help me deal with my permanent departure from this earth. Neither of these apply in my case.

Telling amusing stories from my life experiences gives me pleasure. Over the years I have dabbled at writing about the good, the bad, and the ugly, but I had never gone past twenty pages, because life got in the way.

My stories are based on my growing up in a very large Irish Catholic family, starting my own family, and my brief service in the Army as a military police officer. Some of the stories about my Army days are not unlike those found in the movie and television series *M*A*S*H.*

Every tale I tell is based on the facts as I remember them, but at my age I cannot be totally sure of their accuracy. If you find something in the book to be inaccurate, not true, or you question the timing of the events, please keep it to yourself. Many of the names have been changed in order to protect the innocent and the guilty, or just because I could not remember.

Chapter 1

Like Father, Like Son

I expected our flight from Fort Benning to Oakland to be on a military aircraft. Instead, a chartered old four-engine turboprop was on the runway. The flight attendants looked as if they were old enough to have flown with the Wright brothers.

The captain of the plane called me over to the staging area and said, "I hate to tell you this, Lieutenant, but we can't take off because the plane will be overloaded."

I couldn't believe what I was hearing. Our platoon had been through three months of intense training in preparation for our deployment to Vietnam. We'd been scheduled to ship out two weeks ago, but we kept getting delayed for reasons only the Army knew.

"How do you know the plane will be overloaded?" I asked. He told me they had weighed the complete gear, including a rifle and pistol, rucksack, and two duffel bags for each man. They then extrapolated the total weight for the plane.

I looked at the sample duffel bag on the scale. It was one of mine. I had stocked one of my bags with liquor in order to enjoy a few cocktails on board ship during the cruise to the Orient.

I could just see the headline in the local edition of the *Stars and Stripes*: ARMY MILITARY POLICE LIEUTENANT FACES COURT-MARTIAL FOR ATTEMPTING TO SMUGGLE ALCOHOL ONTO A US ARMY CHARTERED PLANE AND A US NAVY SHIP.

I went over to the scale, picked up my bag, and blurted out: "Captain, this bag is not a valid sample because it contains night-vision equipment." A few more bags holding the usual contents—mostly clothes—were tested for weight, and a new calculation put us just under the limit.

Once on board the plane, we discovered that there was no room for our rucksacks other than underfoot. Seeing this, the flight attendants went on strike and got off the plane. After about a half hour of deliberations, the captain somehow talked them into returning.

I had flown only once before, and it was on a 727 jet on one of my trips from Boston back to MP school at Fort Gordon. I had been nervous on that trip because it was not clear to me how an engine without propellers could stay up in the air. I took comfort in the thought that with this old four-propeller turboprop, we would not fall out of the sky.

With our knees up high over our rucksacks, we headed down the runway. The pilot used every bit of the runway and the plane barely made it over the trees. During the flight our legs were uncomfortable; however, we got a close view of the majestic Rocky Mountains.

When the plane landed at the Oakland Airport, my platoon joined up with the other two platoons in our Military Police Company. We were immediately hustled to the Port of Oakland, where we boarded the USNS *Buckner*. The *Buckner* was a transport vessel that had supported World War II and the Korean War. An Army engineering battalion was already on board.

The ship left the dock after dark. There was very little wind in San Francisco Bay, and the sky was bright with stars. I moved to the fantail of the ship to get a better view of the Golden Gate Bridge and to have a cigarette.

As we sailed, I thought of my father. Twenty-three years earlier, he was on a troop ship that sailed from Oakland to the Orient. My mother gave birth to me in Fort Dix, New Jersey, several days after his ship sailed. My father didn't meet me until I was two and a half years old.

Now I was shipping out with my wife eight months pregnant with our second child. Our first son, Dylan, was nine months old.

My father was Richard Joseph Dobbyn Jr. I am Richard Joseph Dobbyn III. Or in the words of a neighbor, an elderly lady from Italy, "Little Ricky the Turd."

The three-week voyage to Vietnam made me aware of the distinct possibility that I—and a large number of my fellow passengers—would not be returning home. This state of mind prompted many memories—good and not so good—of my past.

Chapter 2

Mom and Dad

*M*y father grew up in Boston and was the third of six children. In 1938, he graduated from the prestigious Boston Latin High School, where he played football and baseball. Along with his excellent academic accomplishments, he had great success as a pitcher. His family took summer vacations in Milton, New Hampshire, where he played in the local industrial baseball league.

When my dad graduated from Boston Latin, he stood about six feet three inches tall but was not very heavy. He earned a full year's scholarship to Lawrence Academy, a preparatory high school in Groton, Massachusetts. The idea was that he would gain weight and strength before entering Holy Cross, where he had a baseball scholarship waiting for him.

When he got to Holy Cross, he pitched well. His family had changed their summer vacation site to Swift's Beach in Wareham, and this allowed him to pitch for the Wareham Gatemen in the Cape Cod Baseball League. This league was scouted heavily and spawned many major league players. Somewhere along the way my father was invited to a tryout with the Chicago White Sox.

My father is third from the left in the second row
on the Boston Latin School basketball team

My mother, Barbara Jean O'Neil, grew up in the Binghamton area of New York. She was the only child of John L. O'Neil "Grampa Neil" and Lillian Davis. When my mother was thirteen years old, her mother died. Grampa Neil remarried when she was still in her teens. Her relation-ship with her stepmother was never very good. It affected the relation-ship with Grampa to the point that they rarely communicated after she left home.

My mother spoke many times about her social life and good times at Bing-hamton High School. She was very proud of leading the band as drum majorette. She went to Binghamton Hospital Nursing School and became a registered nurse.

Mother in high school prom dress

My parents met when my mother was visiting her uncle Francis O'Neil, his wife, Peg, and his daughter Phyllis, at their summer house in Wareham. (Uncle Francie lived year-round in Attleboro, Massachusetts, a small city between Boston and Providence. He was a photographer and was elected mayor of Attleboro right after the war. He ran on a platform to provide more benefits for veterans. He later served in the state senate and as the local postmaster.)

My parents communicated constantly while Mother was in training at the Binghamton Nursing School and my father was at Holy Cross. They got together whenever possible during the school year and spent a lot of time together at Swift's Beach in the summer.

They were married on Thanksgiving Day, November 27, 1942, by a justice of the peace. There was no church wedding because Mother was raised a Presbyterian and the Dobbyn family was Catholic—in those days the Catholic Church severely frowned upon a parishioner marrying someone "outside of the Church." They would have preferred that their son marry a prostitute instead of a Protestant.

The annual Boston College versus Holy Cross football game was held the following Saturday, two days after they married. The newlyweds planned to go to the Cocoanut Grove nightclub in Boston that night to attend a Holy Cross gathering. They did not go because Mother developed a migraine headache.

Mother's migraine headache allowed me and my eight siblings to come into existence. A horrific fire broke out at the Cocoanut Grove that night: 492 people died, and hundreds were injured. The fire was responsible for improving fire safety legislations throughout our country.

My father dropped out of Holy Cross after two and a half years to join the Army during World War II. He qualified for officers' training school, and his major in economics and accounting probably got him into the Quartermaster Corp. He went on active duty on July 15, 1942, and was stationed in Fort Dix, New Jersey.

After he deployed to India, my mother moved back to the Brighton section of Boston, where we lived in an apartment near my paternal grandparents. Mother and I shared the apartment with a friend of hers from South Carolina. In the summer of 1944, we visited her family's summer house on Sullivan's Island.

Mother and me at the beach

My father served under Captain Tom Garvey in the 1106 Quartermaster Company, which operated in the province of Assam in the northeastern part of India. It is in the foothills of the Himalayas on the border with Myanmar, then known as Burma. Their supply mission was in support of cargo-moving aircraft. Specifically, this meant getting supplies flown to the

Chinese Army and the US Army fighting the Japanese in China. They also supplied the troops fighting the Japanese in Burma. The only way to China was to fly over the "Hump," the name for the Himalayas coined by US pilots. Recently I was surprised to learn what a difficult and dangerous operation it was. Following is an excerpt from an article by David Axe, a military correspondent and writer.

> Few people appreciate it today, but for a period of more than three years during World War II, a force of mostly American airmen undertook one of history's most complex—and deadliest—logistical operations, flying thousands of tons of supplies from India over the Himalayas into China in rickety, underpowered cargo planes.
>
> "The world's first strategic airlift," the US Air Force calls it.
>
> These flights over the "Hump" were indispensable to China's war effort against the Japanese, thus a major actor in the Allies ultimate victory. But at a tremendous cost. No fewer than 700 Allied planes crashed or got shot down and 1,200 airmen died.

The Quartermaster troops often flew with the airmen, particularly if they were "air dropping" cargo. My father did some flying over the Hump and developed hearing problems as a result. He was hospitalized twice during his service. First for an appendectomy and then with dengue fever. Like most of his men, he had malaria and dysentery.

He brought home many photographs of the local scene and the indigenous folks. He wrote explanations on the back of the photos. As a child, I distinctly recall my horror at the photos dealing with the before, during, and after of the ceremonial beheading of a goat.

When my father's unit arrived in a village previously occupied by the Japanese, the village chief was pleased to see them. The chief invited him on a tiger hunt. They hunted while riding on elephants. My father killed a tiger with his carbine rifle. He had a rug made and brought it back home with him.

Father with tiger rug

A few of my father's letters to my mother from India were saved, and each one had some poetry. Following is an excerpt from one of those letters:

We went to Mass last Sunday, with a very old Italian priest officiating. It seems that he was a bit afraid to come to our camp because he was from a belligerent country. We got quite a collection of rupees from us for him, and tears came to his eyes as he thanked us and the American people for what they've done and what they are doing. Of course, now he is officially an ally of ours. We were all crowded in a small empty rectangular bamboo hut, and we were sweating like pigs, but nobody minded. It seemed so strange that God could follow us around the world and be in this same native hut with us. The setting and surroundings were so solemn, the thoughts of more than one man could be seen on his face. It wasn't just an ordinary Mass, dear; it seemed to most of us like a special favor bestowed upon us. It means so much more to these Catholic boys— they seemed to have a firm hold on something.

The world has grown so dark with sin,
that God seems far away
But never comes an evening dusk,
when my girl does not pray.
All day men's greed and hate and fear
bring heartaches and despair
But ever when the day is through,
her head is bowed in prayer.
Though tyrant lusts and vain desires
have torn one's faith apart
As surely as the twilight falls,
prayers rise from her true heart.
So much strange terror haunts the night,
and bitterness the day.
But all of life cannot be wrong,
as long as sweethearts pray.

Well, darling, it's fairly good penmanship, anyway.

My father's best friend from childhood, Joe Shea, was in the Army in the European theater. They corresponded throughout the war, and in each letter my father tells Joe how much he loves my mother and how lucky he is to have met her. In one letter, he even goes on a bit about me. He writes that he has dreams of me crashing through the line of Holy Cross's rival, Boston College.

I learned many years later that Joe was the actual FBI agent portrayed in the movie *Catch Me If You Can.*

In November of 1944, First Lieutenant Dobbyn was promoted to company commander.

Lt. Richard J. Dobbyn, receiving Distinguished Service Award for service in China Burma India Theater, World War II.

Father receiving meritorious service award

Chapter 3

One Cat, One Dog, One Tiger, and Five Kids

Dad returned to the States in December 1945. In addition to the tiger rug, he brought ivory-inlaid plaques and a hand-carved folding table also inlaid with ivory. He regretfully reported to my mother that a collection of rubies had been stolen from him on the train in India. He was discharged from active duty in March 1946 and automatically became a member of the Army inactive reserve.

My parents rented a small bungalow in Abington, Massachusetts, a quiet town about twenty miles south of Boston. My brother Dennis joined the family in October. Next came Clarence, the cat. He was a huge yellow Angora. In September of 1947, my sister Christina was born. Also that year, Spooky the dog joined us. She was a mixture of husky and collie and loved to run…all the time.

The bungalow was getting a bit tight for all of us, so we moved into a brand-new development in the Mattapan section of Boston. All the homes were two-floor duplexes. We lived on the first floor and the Currans lived on the second. Veterans with families of Irish descent made up the majority of the residents.

My father worked for the Maine and New Hampshire Theater Co. He traveled extensively through upper New England, distributing films. On weekends, my parents tried to sleep in a bit. I, on the other hand, wanted attention as soon as possible. They placed the tiger rug in the hallway in front of their bedroom. Its mouth was wide open with large white menacing teeth capable of biting my head off. I was scared to death of the thing, but it's presence there meant my parents were able to get more sleep.

My first "ride" was a tricycle. Our house was at the top of a hill, which ended at River Street along the Neponset River. I decided to go down the sidewalk of the hill without using the pedals. Big mistake! The pedals were flying around so fast I couldn't stop them to slow down. As the old saying goes, I went ass over teakettle and whacked my head on the curbstone. I woke up sometime later in my bed with a cold washcloth on my head. As a nurse, my mother was confident that I had a concussion and would wake up eventually. Some would say this incident may have contributed to some of my erratic behaviors later on in life.

My education started in kindergarten at the Edmund P. Tyler Elementary School, located in Mattapan Square, about a half mile from the house. I played one hell of a mean triangle. By the time I was in first grade, Spooky had settled down and started meeting me after school for the walk home. She followed me everywhere. Sometimes the kids living farther up the hill, who we dubbed "O'Toole's Gang," would come down and harass the kids on our street. I don't know why we fought, but we always did. When Spooky sensed I was in danger, she would come barking and growling after my assailant. She never bit, but she never had to. Eventually, I could sic Spooky on anyone by command: "Go get 'em, Spooky!"

My sister Phyllis was born in June of 1949. Mother really had her hands full caring for the four of us, particularly because my father was traveling during the week.

When the Korean War broke out, the Army notified my father that his inactive reserve status was changed to active duty. Mother would have none of it. She organized a little get-together with neighborhood friends the night before his physical. Their good friend Dr. Healey provided the Benzedrine, and my mother supplied the booze. The next day, he was shaking so bad he was declared unfit for active duty.

One of the benefits of my father's job was that we could go downtown to attend private showings of new movies before they were released. We sat in a tiny theater with a couple of other families and watched *Snow White*, *Pinocchio*, and *Fantasia*. For my sixth birthday party, he brought home a projector and a Roy Rogers movie.

There was a small field behind our house, and my father taught me how to block and tackle in football and passed on to me as much of his knowledge about becoming a baseball pitcher as I could absorb. In the fall, kids in the neighborhood would show up. He organized games of football and joined in the play himself. I clearly remember when he had the football and

Me with football pose

challenged all of us to tackle and bring him down before he went over the goal line. He slowly plodded forward with a couple of us on each leg and the others bouncing off him. When he did go down, we all laughed and cheered.

The first movie I ever saw in a regular theater was when I walked by myself to the Oriental Theatre in Mattapan Square, which was a mile away. *Flying Tigers* was playing. The Flying Tigers were American aviators who volunteered to help defend China against the Japanese prior to the United States entering the war. They were recruited under presidential authority but were technically in the Chinese Air Force and operated out of Burma. I wonder if I was allowed to go see it because my father served in Burma, and why he didn't go with me.

I was given twenty cents for the movie and candy. The film had already been running when I sat down with my box of candy. John Wayne starred. I loved watching the planes in their many "dog fights." The American planes had the head of a tiger shark on their noses, and the Japanese pilots were portrayed as despicable, ugly creatures. When the movie ended, I saw that it was going to be shown again. I decided to stay and catch the part of the film I had missed. Then I got wrapped up in it and stayed until the end. It suddenly dawned on me that my parents might be wondering why I was not home yet.

I stupidly thought that by racing home I could dramatically minimize my lateness. I ran out of the theater and into the street in front of a car, which came to a screeching halt inches from me. The driver was horrified and kept asking me if I was okay. I was totally okay physically, but incredibly embarrassed and shaking. When I got home, I didn't get a spanking. Much worse was the guilt they laid on me in the disappointment they expressed.

My sister Polly was born in April of 1951. She was the first sibling whose birth I remember vividly. She had jet-black hair and a very red complexion, unlike her siblings.

All five Dobbyn kids

Halloween was a big deal in our family. Mother went all out making costumes. Each year, a different neighbor on the street would host a Halloween party in their basement for the kids. The year my parents hosted the party, they dressed up as a proper-looking Indian couple. I assume that was based on my father's war experience. The kids had doughnuts and cider and the adults had cocktails. We played games and almost everyone bobbed for apples.

Denny became old enough for the two of us to play together. We competed as a team in "piggyback" wrestling. I carried him on my back, and when we moved in against our opponent, he had to grapple with the other rider and try to topple him over.

We were pretty good; however, in our last match, I went down hard on his leg and broke it. It was a major break and he wore a cast over most of his leg for the next six weeks.

Denny in baby carriage with Father, Chrissy, and two neighborhood girls

One of Boston's nicknames is Beantown, and true to form, every Saturday night we had baked beans and franks with brown bread. I hated beans and refused to eat them. My mother respected this and went heavy for me on the franks and brown bread.

In the winter, we often came in from playing out in the cold to a dinner of pancakes and sausages. The small breakfast sausages were strictly rationed to two sausages per person, and I always craved more. That craving was more than satisfied when I became a self-supporting adult.

Chapter 4

Denial

On a mild, snow-free day in February 1952, when I was in the third grade and walking home from school, I noticed two cars were parked in front of our house. I sped up my pace, curious to see who was visiting us.

When I entered through the front door, Mother came running up to me, sobbing, "Ricky, your father is dead! He's gone, Ricky!"

I blurted out, "Who's going to play ball with me?"

My father was crushed when his car smashed into a train at a railroad crossing in Franklin, Vermont. He was hard of hearing due to his plane trips over the Himalayas. That and a poorly designed crossing may have been responsible for the collision. He died within minutes.

The air at the wake was thick with the sweet, sickening smell of flowers. I knelt in front of the open casket and wondered who the man inside was. I refused to believe the pasty-faced man in a suit and tie, wearing white gloves draped with rosary beads, was my father. My father was not dead. I did not cry.

My mother's uncle Francie sat next to me at the funeral service in Saint Gabriel's in Brighton. As the casket, covered with an American flag, was wheeled by us, he whispered in my ear that I would be given that flag.

He stayed with me for that whole day. He took me to Fort Independence on Boston Harbor. We meandered slowly around the fort. I don't remember anything we talked about, but he kept my mind and feelings away from dipping into the grief that would follow. The politician in Uncle Francie knew what would distract and comfort me. Never trust a politician though, even if he is your own uncle. He never followed through with his promise. I joked with my mother for years that I was still waiting for my flag. Late in her life, she covered for Uncle Francie by presenting me with a triangular box containing a folded American flag with my father's war medals resting on it.

Night after night for weeks I cried myself to sleep, and every day I looked to see if Dad's white Ford was parked out front. It very slowly came to me that I would never see him again.

At school, I was embarrassed that I was the only kid in my class who did not have a father. After the Pledge of Allegiance, the class sang "My Country 'Tis of Thee." When we got to the part "land where our fathers died," I felt like everyone was staring at me.

Mother's grief totally consumed her for a very long time. She would often forget where she was or where she was going. Along with losing her mother at an early age, she now had lost the love of her life. The prospect of raising five kids ranging in age from eight to one was overwhelming.

At the funeral service, several people had come up to me and said: "Ricky, you are now *the man of the house.*" It was said in a way that sounded like I would be taking on some major responsibilities. I felt very important, but then I had no idea what those responsibilities could be.

It turned out that keeping track of Mother when she got disoriented was one of them. The other was minding my siblings when she had to leave us alone, which thankfully, was not very often.

Over the next couple of years, the details and accomplishments of my father's life were made known to me. My father was a superb role model, bordering on sainthood. Growing up, I constantly strived to be like him. I think the letter that my uncle Jack wrote about my father may help you understand the large pair of shoes I tried to fill.

> Dick had a great year at Lawrence Academy. First of all, he didn't have to study at all. Having survived and graduated from Latin School, he was able to get all As without cracking a book. The Latin teacher would have Dick conduct the class if he was absent. He played all sports. He was an end on the football team. He played varsity basketball, although he had never played it before. Basketball was not played in Boston schools until 1945. It was done away with in the 1920s. It was considered too rough. They allowed football and hockey. To some this might seem illogical, and it was. He played tennis, although he did not own a racket. In the school championship, he came in second, beaten by the fellow he borrowed the racket from.

See what I mean? While in hindsight it was good for me to have goals, it was depressing when I always fell short of what he had accomplished.

Chapter 5

The Aftershock

My mother's mental state was very much adrift, and although she could struggle through the basic requirements of running a household, she lacked experience in all things financial. Papa Dobbyn, my grandfather, was well equipped to help in this area. He was a self-taught accountant with a high school degree from Boston Latin and held various financial positions for Joseph Kennedy and family. At this time, he was the treasurer for Joe Kennedy's film-distribution company. No-nonsense and gruff, he loved golf and poker and crocheted in his spare time.

My grandfather negotiated a small settlement with the railroad company over my father's death, managed Mother's money, and even helped her balance the checkbook. There was a small life insurance policy and social security benefits, but all in all, money was pretty tight. It would have been even tighter if Papa hadn't finagled a three-bedroom apartment in a subsidized housing project only a fifteen-minute walk from his house. It was also ten minutes to Saint Gabriel's Elementary School.

The housing project did not allow pets, so Clarence and Spooky were not permitted to join us. I was crushed. I was somewhat assuaged when my mother explained that the Garvey family volunteered to take Spooky, with the proviso that she could join us again when our circumstances changed. I don't remember who took Clarence, but I do remember that the Currans told us he showed up once at their house and had to be returned to his new home.

Our building was on Commonwealth Avenue—one of the main roads and trolley lines feeding downtown. It had an elevator and was six stories high. We lived on the fifth floor, and from our apartment we could see all of downtown and the famous giant neon Citgo sign in Kenmore Square. To this day, the sign can be viewed from home plate at Red Sox games at Fenway Park.

There was an elevator and a garbage chute on each floor. My brother Denny and I were afraid of the elevator, and our sisters Chrissy and Phyllis were terrified by it. If some jackass jumped up high and came down hard, the elevator would stop. The big red emergency button that summoned the fire department was getting worn out from overuse. To rescue us, the firemen opened the door to the elevator shaft on the floor above and climbed down a ladder to the top of the elevator. They opened the hatch on the top of the elevator to check if we were okay and then started the elevator.

Properly monitoring the activities of five young children from the fifth floor was an impossible task for my mother. I was old enough to go out on my own, but Mother never knew where I was. Denny was allowed to hang out with me but, like Chrissy and Phyllis, was not allowed to leave the building on his own. Polly got outside with my mother in her baby carriage. They all spent a lot of time in front of the TV.

The Saint

I was enrolled in Saint Gabriel's to finish off the third grade. Catechism classes, prayers, and hymns were added to my curriculum. John Philip Sousa's marching music was played as we moved around the school in single file to recess and lunch. I liked that.

Mother leaned heavily on her faith and elevated herself from Catholic to super-Catholic. I joined in under the guidance and instruction of the good sisters at Saint Gabriel's.

I wanted to be the best Catholic in the world. I started attending Mass by myself almost every morning. I was given a daily missal, which contains specific readings in Latin and English for every day of the year, for each section of the Mass, and for whatever saint is being recognized. It had a black leather binding and several colored ribbons to help you flip to the proper pages. I remember trying hard to find the correct reading for each day in order to keep up with the priest. I never really figured it out. Learning how to score a baseball game is much easier than using the missal.

Just for the hell of it, I recently went on YouTube and looked up "How to use the Roman Catholic daily missal." I still couldn't follow how to use it. I am quite sure that the narrator, always looking away from the camera to the teleprompter, had no clue either. She concluded her lesson by stating, "If you still have a problem, there is a section in the missal on how to use the missal."

I joined the Saint Gabriel's choir and enjoyed singing the Mass in Gregorian chant. There are no breaks in Gregorian chant, so everyone has to breathe at different times. The nuns taught us how to read Gregorian chant music. It was a different system than is used in modern times. The choirmaster had written his own Mass in today's music. He played a monstrous organ, and we sang in Latin. For some reason, he considered me a good singer and selected me to sing a hymn to the Mother Mary at the Sunday eleven o'clock High Mass.

I sang too softly and constantly went off-key. I am not a good singer. I envied the altar boys because they did not have to attend rehearsals and got paid for weddings and funerals. Of course, today we know that working closely with a priest might be quite dangerous.

At the height of my attempted sainthood, I believed that I would be given extra points for whatever suffering and pain I could endure during my religious practices. This belief was derived from reading books about the lives of the saints.

The nuns encouraged us to drop into church anytime to visit the Lord and the saints. One Saturday afternoon, I set out for Saint Gabriel's in an absolute downpour. As I splashed through the puddles, I confidently smiled to myself that the Lord must be well aware of what a wonderful Catholic I was. I was totally drenched and shivering when I entered the church. There was no one there. I decided to worship Mother Mary and knelt down at the shrine next to the main altar.

My hubris got the best of me when I decided that I was due some kind of a sign from above. I stared at Mother Mary's eyes, praying hard that she would send me a sign from above. This was not unprecedented since she had already appeared to some European kids in Lourdes, France, and in Fatima, Portugal. Just a quick wink of the eye would have done it for me. When nothing happened, I totally gave up on my quest for sainthood.

War Games

There was a vacant lot behind a row of stores next to our building. The lot was overgrown with weeds, bushes, and some small trees. A large dead tree lay in the middle of the lot. This was the playground for the kids in our building. The dead tree became a ship, a castle, or a fort. We used peach baskets or trash can covers as shields and broomstick handles as swords or guns. Bows and arrows were made from the tree limbs. Clumps of pulled weeds served as bombs or grenades.

We had intense battles as pirates, cowboys and Indians, knights of the realm, and World War II soldiers. My favorite game was a contest to see who could die the best. A death could take up to a minute as one staggered around, fell down, struggled back up and fired back at the enemy one more time.

At some point, our group and some other project kids put together a football team. On Saturdays we marched a little over a mile to a field at Cleveland Circle. We played the local team tackle without much equipment. I did at least have a leather helmet.

The referee was usually someone who emerged from the bar across the street, and our time clock was on a billboard over the stores. To this day, I am amazed at how our games came together without any—or very little—adult supervision.

Roughly that same group played tag project-style. We met Friday afternoons, and one of us was chosen to be "it." The game lasted all weekend. When the one who was it tagged someone, that person had to help him chase everyone else. The game ended when we all had been tagged, or by five o'clock Sunday night.

One day I was being chased through the first floor of my building. I opened the door to the stairs and turned right toward the basement. I cleared the steps to a landing. The kid chasing me was right on my tail, ready to tag me. Ahead of me was a very long set of stairs leading to the basement. I jumped.

Halfway down the stairs, my head hit the part of the ceiling that jutted out. I landed on my back and tumbled to the bottom. Blood was gushing from my head and pouring down my face and clothes.

The doctor in the emergency room didn't have to use any local anesthetic to sew me up because my head was still numb from the trauma. The wound was in my hairline. I looked pretty silly with this rectangular boxy white bandage on my head.

Even if I had not hit the ceiling, I never would have come close to clearing the stairs and landing properly. I think I had too much adrenaline in my system and panicked. It was really a stupid move. In Vietnam, I often acted first and thought later. This had mixed results.

On My Honor I Will Do My Best

When I was nine years old, I joined the Cub Scouts with great enthusiasm. The uniforms they wore pretty sharp looking, and I was eager to go hiking and camp in the woods.

The first meeting was held at the den mother's apartment with four or five Cubs. The meeting started with our standing up and reciting the Cub Scout Oath. Then we were each given a piece of wood to take home. The assignment was to sand and stain the wood, then glue pasta alphabet letters onto the wood, spelling out...I forget what. Then we had milk and cookies. On my way out, the den mother gave me a pamphlet on how to attain the rank of Bear.

I found the assignment tedious and boring. I couldn't paste the pasta on straight. I read the steps required to become a Bear and they didn't interest me, nor did the steps to become a Webelo. I went to a couple more meetings, mainly just for the milk and cookies. I saved my mother the expense of buying a uniform.

Uncle Jack

My father was the third of the six Dobbyns. His two older siblings were Mary and Alice, and following him were Ethel, John (Jack), and Philip (Phil). At this time, Uncle Jack was pursuing a career as a Catholic priest. He had a quick wit and a very dry sense of humor. He told me many years later that my father's death had influenced his decision to become a priest.

Jack was very helpful to my mother and us kids. He took me to see a Boston Braves game, and also took all of us to the Boston Garden to see the Ice Capades and the Ringling Bros. & Barnum and Bailey Circus.

When I was ten, he brought me to the Little League sign-up. He looked around the room and said, "Ricky, I don't think you are going to make it." I think he was softening the blow because there were many athletic eleven- and twelve-year-old kids competing against me. He was right; I didn't make it, but I was able to join the minor league team with uniforms that looked just like major league teams.

My fielding ability was hampered because I had my father's old glove. It looked nothing like the other boys' gloves. It had no webbing and only a deep pocket in the middle. I had a great pitching windup and threw a dangerously fast ball, which only rarely went over the plate.

Sinner

I started hanging out with Jimmy Donati, who lived in the building next to ours. He was a couple of years older than me and just looked like someone you did not want to mess with. His well-greased jet-black hair was brushed back, and he liked to put his shirt collar up.

There was a Laundromat, a bar, and a delicatessen next to our building. Across the street from the deli was a drugstore. Jimmy and I started shoplifting from both stores. It didn't really matter to us what we stole. It was basically just the thrill, but the candy was a real bonus. Eventually, whenever I went into any store, I would try to pocket something.

Mother got me a used two-wheeler. This expanded my opportunities to get in trouble. There was a bicycle shop in Brighton Center. Jimmy had a plan. We parked our bikes right in front of the store. I went inside first and went up to the counter, occupying the owner with questions about the cost of this or that. Jimmy came in behind me and lifted some accessories for our handlebars. I joined him outside, and instead of racing away, for some reason we stayed right there to affix the horns, bells, and streamers to our bikes. The owner saw us and came flying out the door. We ran, pushing the bikes and then jumping on them to escape. I could hear the owner yelling at us as we quickly pedaled away.

There was a slaughterhouse near Brighton Center. The first time I went there was with Jimmy. We sneaked inside and saw how the cows' throats were cut. I was horrified. I visited a few more times but never went inside. I stayed outside and watched the cows in the corral. I remember that one of the boys with me climbed up and jumped onto the back of a cow for a ride. He slid off and fell into a pile of cow dung.

Our adventures started to take on more of a deeper criminal aspect. We went to the junkyard and scavenged bicycle parts. The idea was to make a bike that looked like it worked. The plan was to crash the bike into a car just as it was stopping at a red light. Then hit the driver up for cash.

Evidently, reports of my bad behavior made it home because my mother started talking about reform school. In desperation, she sought out the help of Papa Dobbyn and arranged for me to meet with him.

With great trepidation, I went to his house and sat down with him at the kitchen table. He was puffing on his Lucky Strike cigarette while he explained the bad things that would happen to me if I did not straighten out my act. As an incentive, he gave me a baseball signed by all the Red Sox, including my hero, Ted Williams. He also gave me a Timex wristwatch. I got out of there respectfully, with no intention of straightening out my act.

Chapter 6

Swift's Beach

*M*other put aside enough money to get us out of the projects for the summer. She rented the same cottage at Swift's Beach for the summers of 1953 and 1954. Papa Dobbyn always rented a large two-story cottage next to the ocean. We didn't have a car, so my grandparents shuttled us there and helped Mother get around.

One time I rode alone with Papa from Boston to the beach. I was still very intimidated by him and afraid to tell him I had to take a whiz. I just let it trickle down my leg into my shoes. He didn't know until we arrived at the beach. He was astounded that I hadn't said a word.

Our cottage was a couple of blocks away from the water. Ours and most of the cottages there had rooms with partitions open to the rafters. Everyone had a screened-in porch in the front. The landlord, Mr. O'Brien, had a small cottage behind us, which he used on weekends. He was an older gentleman with a potbelly who always wore a bathing suit and smoked or chewed cigars.

Family picture at Swift's Beach with Spooky visiting

Mr. O'Brien kept a rowboat in the marshes behind his lot. He showed me how to caulk and paint the bottom and let it soak for a day or two to let the floorboards swell up and not leak.

All the boats along the marsh were kept afloat despite the level of tide. It was similar to a clothesline setup. An iron pole was placed offshore and a stake was placed on the marsh. A line was strung through a pulley on the pole and then back to the stake. The boat was kept in the deep water near the pole and pulled in to get on board. That little system fascinated me.

After the boat was in the water for a couple of days, the floorboards swelled up and the boat no longer leaked. Mr. O'Brien then took me out and showed me how to row. On our way back to the house, he said the boat was mine for as long as I wanted and to take good care of it. I could not believe what I was hearing. My own boat!

I rowed that boat all over the small bay in the marshes. I would row out against the wind and then use one oar on the stern as a tiller to "skull" back with the wind. Sometimes Mother would pile us all into the boat. We would row around and go to the small island in the bay to collect shells and driftwood. She loved driftwood.

I became hooked on boats, and I thank and blame Mr. O'Brien for costing me thousands of dollars sunk into sailboats and powerboats over the years. They've brought me great pleasure and some terrifying moments.

The Hero

One day I was walking out on the marsh that ran along the side of the beach and came upon a couple of kids who were watching a boy thrashing up and down in the water several yards from shore. He was in over his head and went under, then pushed off the bottom to come up for air. The onlookers thought nothing of it, but I knew he would not be able to bob his way back into the marsh. I jumped off the marsh, and due to my height was able to tiptoe out to the boy. I extended my hand when he surfaced, and he grabbed it. I was able to pull him back to the marsh.

He told me he was indeed close to drowning and insisted that I go back to the beach with him and meet his mother. On the way I had visions of everyone gathering around and thanking me for the heroism I displayed in saving the boy's life. I thought maybe I would be in the paper, or mentioned on the radio. We ran up to his mother, who was sunning on a blanket.

He loudly blurted out: "Mommy, this kid saved my life. I almost drowned."

She said: "That's fine, dear. We have to pack up now."

I guess she didn't believe him. That really burst my balloon.

The Entertainers

My uncle Phil, the youngest Dobbyn, was different from his brothers in that athletics did not interest him. He was more interested in photography and music, particularly bluegrass. Outgoing with a quirky sense of humor, he had fun spoofing complete strangers.

When the Dobbyns gathered together at Papa and Grammy Dobbyn's home for Thanksgiving and Christmas, he recorded the events with his movie camera, entertaining all his nieces and nephews with his humor, even sitting at the little kids' table with us.

He spent the summers at Swift's Beach while he was still in school. As is the case with the youngest in most families, he could get away with a lot more than his siblings and was not at all intimidated by Papa; in fact, he seemed to enjoy teasing him. He caddied for Papa Dobbyn on weekends at the Pocasset Golf Club.

There was a community building at Swift's Beach where the residents regularly had a spaghetti dinner and dance night. The sauce was prepared by an Italian family and was wonderful. Uncle Phil was the DJ. He would go around and get people of all ages off their seats and onto the dance floor, saying, "If you can walk, you can dance!"

With just his voice and the mic, he banged out the Mexican Hat Dance, the Bunny Hop, the Hokey Pokey, and the Conga.

I can hear him now bellowing, "One, two, three, la Conga!" as the line of dancers snaked their way around the room.

At the end of the night he led us all singing: "Hail, hail, the gang's all here, what the heck do we care" from the comic opera *The Pirates of the Penzance.*

Swift's Beach had a commercial district owned by Mr. Voss called Voss City. At the Variety Store, one could have fried clams for lunch and buy groceries, newspapers, and magazines, candy, souvenirs, beach balls, and the like. There was a dance hall, which played music day and night, and an arcade with pinball machines. There was also the outdoor theater, which showed movies several nights a week. And of course, there was Voss Realty.

The outdoor theater had an amateur night, and Phil insisted I get onstage. He had me practice "I'm Looking Over a Four-Leaf Clover" every day for a week.

All the wooden folding chairs in the theater were full and yet I was not even the slightest bit nervous. I banged out the tune completely off-key and was awarded a large Baby Ruth candy bar. I think it was the fact that I had practiced the song hundreds of times that kept me calm.

Crime Doesn't Pay…Much

I developed a minor addiction to supplement my petty-theft career: pinball! My mother would give me money to pick up groceries at Voss's market. I siphoned off enough of the change to stop by the arcade and play pinball.

I finally got caught stealing. A family that lived at Swift's Beach year-round were our next-door neighbors. I hung out with their son, Ralph. He was a couple of years older than me. He taught me how to fish off the marsh with a hand line and how to bait a milk bottle with bread to catch minnows, which we then sold to the fishermen.

He liked girlie magazines and would let me peruse them. We both got nabbed in Voss City trying to replenish his supply. The Variety Store manager turned us in to my mother and his parents. Mother was absolutely shocked, and I was humiliated, not so much about stealing, but rather what I stole.

My sister Chrissy hung out with Ralph's sister and picked up a case of lice from her, which was passed around the family. The house smelled of vinegar for days, and Chrissy's long, curly blond hair was cut short. She never again let it grow beyond her shoulders.

The Shit Storm

In the middle of the summer of '54, I was hospitalized for a week with pneumonia. I suffered numerous attacks on my buttocks from hypodermic needles filled with penicillin, which had become broadly available in the 1940s. Without it, I would have died. My life in any past generation would have been brief. I consider myself very lucky.

My hospital room had four beds. Two were empty, and there was an old man across the room from me. He hardly spoke and lay there with his mouth wide open, usually snoring loudly.

I was reading a comic book when I heard a splat sound on my bed. The old fella was attacking me with his own feces. I laid out my comics over the bed and held up one to deflect direct hits on me. He ate very little, so he must having been saving up for days because it was a lengthy shit storm. When a nurse came in, I caught holy hell because I didn't use the call button. I think I forgot because I was having too much fun manning my comic-book fort.

A Visit from Carol

My mother met Mr. Mattson and his family on the beach. He was a widower with four children, three girls around our age and the youngest a boy called Bubba. He rented a cottage next to the beach for the month of August. I believe he and Mother had dinner a couple of times.

The first indication that is was not going to be a very nice day was when I opened the door of the fridge to get some milk for my cereal and heard a very loud bang! I thought the refrigerator had exploded, but it was the sound of a tree smashing the side of the cottage.

Hurricane Carol swept through the New England southern coast on that day, August 31, 1954. It produced a fourteen-foot storm surge. Entire coastal communities were wiped out and the cities of Providence and New Bedford were ten feet underwater. Sixty-five people died and more than a thousand were injured.

A couple of weeks after the storm, my mother wrote to her grandfather.

> *Dear Gramp, just a note to tell you about our escape from Hurricane Carol. We barely escaped with our lives. We left about 10 to 15 minutes before the big tidal wave hit. Our cottage and my mother-in-law's were demolished*

under six feet of water. I happened to be minding a neighbor's four children and a boxer dog. We had to leave when the water came up to our front and back doors.

I started out on foot with 9 children and the dog. Trees were falling all around us, and picnic tables were flying thru the air, and when I took Polly's hand and led her outside, she flew right up in the air like a flag. There was a car that picked us up, and we spent the day safely at the Wareham Town Hall, till someone else drove 14 of us all in one car to Boston. We arrived home without a stitch of clothing except the wet ones we had on. I was barefoot.

We took everything to the beach, for the weather is either very hot or cool there. I went down the next day to salvage what I could and managed to find more than what I expected, but I still lost about $200 worth of stuff as it was, the rest was all mud & muck. I sent 80 lbs. to the laundry and I washed thirteen loads myself. Had bought all their new school clothes there. New shoes wedged in mud under the linoleum. What a terrible mess. It was unnerving enough, but the work of salvaging was physically exhausting. I could not get a car within two blocks of our place, so had to lug it all up in a little red cart, over rooftops in the street and other rubble, etc.

I don't think I will ever be rested again, still I am thankful none were hurt or killed. It seemed the storm gave 101 mphs and lots of damage in Boston, but in our own "Bastille" we were perfectly safe. The children hated to come back, such an adjustment after so much freedom. Am working at a new move now and will let you know when it works out. Let Dad see this letter when he gets home. I don't think I will write another letter, there is so much to do...

Took some snaps, but the rolls are in a drugstore in Wareham to be developed. They may have been lost in the storm. The whole town was flooded. Two big stores burned down during the flood. Well, let's hope we have no more hurricanes, at least till next year. The children got quite a fright, Polly waking up crying. Let's hear from you again, Best love, Jean.

The four children she was minding were Mattson's kids and the boxer was theirs. The new move she was contemplating was no doubt related to her new relationship with Mr. Mattson. He owned Mattson Realty in Providence.

All the money I made caddying for Papa Dobbyn I'd saved in a tin Band-Aid box hidden in the rafters of the cottage. It was lost in the wreckage. The lesson I learned and practiced for many years was to never save any money.

Chapter 7

Moving on Up!

I was eleven years old when we moved to Providence. A rented bungalow in South Providence was our new home. Mother was incredibly relieved to get us out of the projects of Boston. A few more years there and I would have probably been locked up.

As promised, the Garveys returned Spooky to us. When she came in the house, she ran around us like a puppy, jumping for joy.

It was great to have more living space, a front porch, and our own backyard. We were on a quiet street that bordered the beautiful Roger Williams Park. The park had connecting ponds, walking trails, playgrounds, a zoo, a museum, a planetarium, and a carousel.

During winters, we skated on the ponds and went sledding on the small hills. I started playing ice hockey. Chrissy reported that she saw a man exposing himself but that Phyllis didn't see the flasher due to her bad eyesight…She eventually had to wear glasses. After hearing that, I made sure the girls were never alone in the park.

Mother bought an old used Ford sedan. I have a good sense of direction and often served as her navigator in the new city.

She and Mr. Mattson were dating, so the daughter of a Greek family across the street "babysat" and happily kept us entertained by teaching us the latest dance craze, the Jitterbug.

My mother and Mr. Mattson appeared to get along well, but they stopped seeing each other. My guess is there were too many children involved.

I spent the latter half of the sixth grade in the Henry Barnard public school. It was much more relaxed than Saint Gabriel's, and classes were much smaller. They also had music and dance classes. I learned to square dance and played the bass drum in the school band. At recess in the schoolyard, everyone was singing "Rock Around the Clock" by Bill Haley & His Comets. Rock 'n' roll was being born.

Although three years younger than me, Denny was a great playmate. There was a vacant lot with an abandoned building at the end of our street. Since we lacked a playground in our area and had no funds for equipment, we needed to be resourceful. We played basketball with a soccer-sized rubber ball and shot into a peach basket nailed to the building. We set the basket low so we both could dunk. We also set up a golf course with three holes made from tin cans. A salesman in the used-car lot across the street gave us a ball and an old three-iron.

Our house was close to the Cranston city line and was midway between St. Michael's School in Providence and Saint Paul School in the Edgewood section of Cranston. Edgewood was a much better neighborhood and the church was Gothic architecture built of stone. St. Michaels was a much older parish with a drab redbrick church. In the fall, we were all enrolled in Saint Paul School.

That summer I made the Little League team. I played as a

pitcher and a catcher. As a pitcher, I led the league in strikeouts and in batters walked. As a batter, I led the league in home runs and in strikeouts. Despite my extremes, I still made the All-Star Team.

Chapter 8

Dr. and Mrs. Collins

Mother continued her religious fervor; in fact, she met my stepfather, Joseph W. Collins, at a Saint Paul Legion of Mary meeting. (Members of the Legion of Mary met weekly to pray and were active helping those in need throughout the parish.)

Joe grew up in Syracuse, New York. He had earned a bachelor's degree from Niagara University and his masters and doctorate degrees in chemistry from Syracuse University. He worked for Arnold, Hoffman & Company in Providence as a research chemist and drove a cool-looking Mercury.

One day Mother sat me down at the kitchen table and said she had good news. She told me that she and Joe were going to be married. I was flabbergasted, but I kept that quiet. I liked Joe and considered him a good friend, but a father? The thought had never crossed my mind.

Their marriage took place in Saint Paul in 1956. Shortly after, Joe legally adopted the five of us. As part of the adoption process, I had to appear in court to tell the judge whether I wanted me and my siblings to keep the name Dobbyn or take the Collins name. I was opposed to changing names for two reasons of equal importance to me. First, I felt changing our surname would be a betrayal of the memory of our father. Second, I was very self-conscious, and in school I was already known as the kid without a father. In no way did I want to explain a name change.

Mother and Joe bought a large, older house in the Edgewood neighborhood of Cranston. It had three floors and a finished basement.

Denny and I shared the room on the third floor, which was reached by a narrow, twisting staircase. It granted us a lot of privacy and we could listen to the radio at all hours and not disturb anyone. We did our homework listening to the Boston Celtics games and cheering loudly.

There was a master bedroom and three other bedrooms on the second floor. Chrissy had her own room and Phyllis and Polly shared a room. The only bathroom was also on the second floor and had a tub but no shower. We all bathed weekly, on Saturday nights, with Phyllis and Polly bathing together. These arrangements changed dramatically over the next few years. My brother Stephen arrived in 1957. Vinny was born in 1959, Mark in 1961, and Bobbie in 1963. The grand total was nine, five boys and four girls.

Joe took me with him to a Niagara vs. UConn basketball game and several stock car races. His favorite sporting event of the year was the Indie 500. He grew up next to a golf course and caddied throughout his youth. Eventually, he took up the sport and became an accomplished golfer. He rarely had the chance to play much golf as a father and stepfather. Many years later, while visiting from Florida, I joined him and Denny for a round of golf. Joe had not been playing more than once or twice a year and still shot beautifully. Stealing from "The Parable of the

Talents" in the Bible about a man with many talents, I told him that if he didn't start playing golf regularly, he would be sinfully wasting a God-given talent.

Our basketball court was upgraded from the peach basket to a real backboard and net over the garage. Denny and I played stoopball on the front steps and Wiffle ball in the driveway. We added color to our games by pretending we were a certain pro player or team. He was always the Red Sox; I was the Yankees, because I chose to follow in Papa Dobbyn's footsteps. He shunned the Red Sox after the owner traded Babe Ruth to the Yankees. (A few years later, I came to my senses and became a loyal Red Sox fan.)

All of us played games of touch football in the side yard. One time I slipped the ball under the back of Phyllis's shirt, and she snuck into the end zone for a touchdown.

Bless Me Father for I Have Sinned

My mother and Joe remained rabid Catholics. Whether we liked it or not, every night we got out our rosary beads, got on our knees in the living room, and prayed in unison. The rosary took a long time and was eventually moved to the kitchen, where we prayed while washing and drying the dishes and cleaning up after dinner.

We lit candles on the Advent wreath every week in December leading up to Christmas. In the spring, during the six weeks of Lent, we had to totally abstain from something we really favored, such as candy or a favorite TV show. We made the Stations of the Cross almost daily. On Good Friday, we were encouraged to be completely silent from noon to three o'clock, the hours Jesus was dying on the cross. The seriousness of this occasion apparently escaped me and my friends, because we used this time as an opportunity to silently goad each other into breaking the silence by saying something.

Of course, Sunday Mass was year-round and was never missed, and we were scared into going to confession regularly. We were afraid of dying and going to hell for having committed a mortal sin. It seemed like *everything* was a mortal sin. On Saturday afternoons, the monsignor and a younger priest heard confessions. Our monsignor was old and hard of hearing. Everyone tried to have the younger priest hear their confession because the monsignor whispered very loud and could be heard by everyone in the church. When the monsignor ran out of confessors, he would come out of the confessional and hijack some of us who were in line for the young priest. Not only would his reactions to your transgressions be heard by everyone, but he always gave out more prayers to say for penance.

One Saturday afternoon several of us went to the movies, and when we got out, we realized that if we ran, we could get to church before five, when confessions closed. We arrived a little before five and only the monsignor was on duty. I was first in. "You just came from the movies, didn't you?" he yelled. He went on about how he was sick and tired of kids racing in from the movies at closing time. We must have been making him late for dinner. I confessed to disobeying my parents and having impure thoughts: and my penance was to say the whole rosary. I believed this to be cruel and unusual punishment related to my showing up late.

Saint Paul School went from the first to the ninth grade. Each classroom had about fifty students versus the twenty or so in public schools. Two desks were pushed together in each aisle to fit everyone in the room. Uniforms were mandatory. Boys wore blue shirts and ties. Girls wore blue jumpers and white blouses. Sister Macarious was our seventh-grade teacher. She was on the verge of retirement and had little patience for those who messed around in class. She was small in stature and was ambidextrous. She could deliver a painful whack to the head with either hand.

Athletics

My seventh-grade classmate Don Daley had grown up in Saint Paul School. He was an outgoing guy and we hit it off right away. We shared a love of sports, and he recruited me to play football on Saturday mornings at Meadows Field. Like the football I played in Boston, there was no adult supervision. Don also got me involved in basketball. The city sponsored a Saturday-morning program at Park View Junior High. Two basketball-savvy teachers ran the program. I had only played basketball with Denny in the driveway. My winter sport had been playing hockey outdoors on ponds.

Don was around five feet six inches tall and I was around six feet. He was already a good player and could dribble and shoot very well. I was what they call a "big stiff"—awkward and clumsy. However, I got very good at rebounding and was smart enough to get the ball to those who could put it in the basket.

Awards were given out at the end of the year and were published in the local fish wrapper. Don won "Best Player." I was very happy to be awarded "Best Attitude."

The Entrepreneur

There was an Episcopal church about a mile from our house, and they had a small gym next to the church. I had watched Joe play basketball there with some guys from work. I found out that the local Boy Scout troop held their weekly Friday-night meetings there. After the meeting they played basketball. Despite my previous very brief experience with the Cub Scouts, I decided to join the Boy Scouts. I figured if I tolerated the Boy Scout requirements, I could play basketball and get out of the house on a Friday night. What really convinced me was that I would be eligible to go to the Boy Scout summer camp for a week. I did the minimum required to show progress toward attaining the rank of Tenderfoot and couldn't wait for the meetings to end and to begin playing basketball.

A week at Camp Yawgoog was not very expensive, so my mother signed me up. The camp was on a lake and we slept in a barracks-like building. Morning activities were always active, like swimming, canoeing, or hiking, all of which I loved. The Girl Scout camp was on the other side of the lake. So you know we had to paddle over that way to wave at the girls. After lunch we had two hours of arts and crafts. I found weaving plastic laces called gimp into a bracelet and the like very boring, but whittling and chopping wood was much more interesting. In the middle of the week we did our overnight camping trip. I had been warned that we would have to eat dehydrated food. Also, my scoutmaster had told me that I had to start a fire without matches if I wanted to earn my promotion to Tenderfoot.

I didn't want to eat the dehydrated food, so before we left on our trip, I went to the small store on the camp grounds to see what they had to eat. I was going to buy just a couple of hot dogs, but then it dawned on me that a lot of my fellow troopers also would prefer hot dogs. I bought an eight-pack of "tube steaks," a loaf of bread, and asked for a pack of matches.

As we marched off to our campsite, I let it be known that for a small price hot dogs were available for dinner. When we arrived, I immediately told our counselor that I needed to build a fire without matches to obtain my promotion to Tenderfoot. He said to let him know and he would check it out. I gathered a pile of twigs and a couple of branches. I rubbed the branches together for a very long time and did not get a single spark. I looked around and nobody was looking my way. I took out the matches and got a number of twigs to catch fire. I called the counselor over and he quickly glanced at the glowing twigs and said he would sign my Tenderfoot worksheet when we went back to the camp.

I gathered a lot more kindling and cranked up the fire. I ate two hot dogs and sold six. In the fall I found a much better place to play basketball, so I resigned from the Scouts and never did get beyond Tenderfoot.

Dirty Player

Next to Saint Paul Church was the Saint Paul "Old Church," a wooden building converted into a basketball court. I played on the Saint Paul CYO (Catholic Youth Organization) league team. I never quite understood why we huddled together before each game to pray to Jesus to help us beat the other Catholic team when Jesus had to be rooting for both of us.

On weekends, we hung out at the Old Church and played pickup games all day long. Long shots often hit the rafters, and if you shot a layup on the run and ran out of bounds, you had to be careful not to wrap yourself around the iron poll supporting the upstairs choir loft.

I was getting to be an overly aggressive player. I had grown another inch or two and played center. I quickly learned that basketball was a contact sport.

The Blessed Sacrament team had a center who must have stayed back in school several times. He was big and muscular and could pass as a twenty-two-year-old. The first time we played, he continually jabbed me with his elbows and was pushing me off-balance when we went up for a rebound.

I finally found an opportunity to retaliate when he caught a pass at midcourt and was dribbling hard to the basket. I was on his tail, and when he went up in the air for a layup, I pushed him hard in the back. He missed the shot and smashed into that pole under the choir loft.

I was ejected from the game and went home. The next morning, Don told me that after the game, Blessed Sacrament guys were looking all over for me and that a brawl was avoided once they could not find me.

Make-Out Mission

"Making out" in the mind of thirteen-year-old boy in Saint Paul's grammar school in 1956 meant at a minimum kissing a girl and at a maximum heavy petting. Neither Don nor I had ever *made out* with a girl. In fact, we were not totally sure what was involved in heavy petting, except that Sister Macarious told us it was a major or even a mortal sin.

Don and I had been going to the CYO Sock Hop every Friday night. We never danced nor were we ever asked to, which was a good thing because we didn't know how. The Jitter Bug was still the rage then. We just hung out drinking Cokes, slipping outside occasionally to sneak a cigarette. Afterward, we went to the local diner and ordered a large fries. At least we got out of the house.

On one such night, Don mentioned that he thought Diane in our class was cute. He proposed that I ask Diane's friend Lois to go to the movies with him and Diane. The girls agreed to go to the Saturday matinee with us. I did not really have a romantic attraction for Lois. No matter. We were determined to make out.

We met the girls inside the theater. We picked out seats in the back and most remote part of the room. Lois was as frightened as I was. We tried to converse and were both extremely relieved when the film started.

After about thirty minutes, I managed to slip my arm along the back of her chair. After another fifteen minutes, I let my hand drop softly onto her shoulder. She did not react adversely to my touch. After about ten minutes, I thought, Okay, this is it; time to go in for a kiss. I awkwardly leaned over, lightly pulled her toward me, and tried to give her a kiss. She was not at all aware of my intentions and our teeth clashed loudly into each other.

Lois was good about it in that she did not say anything, slap me, or get up to leave, but our date was over and I did not make out!

Rats and Eels

The Providence River was only a couple of blocks away from our house, where there was an abandoned shipyard and a yacht club. A section of the shipyard had been converted into a drive-in movie theater. The docks were still in place, and an inactive WWII submarine was tied up for use by the Naval Reserve Center. On weekends, it was open for free and we were frequent visitors.

I cannot remember how I met Bill Lacasse, probably while skimming rocks along the waterfront. Bill lived a couple of blocks away in an old house on the river, next to the shipyard. He was an adventuresome type with a strong Tarzan-like build.

He had a leaky old rowboat that required two of us to operate, one to row and the other to bail. We rowed out to the middle of the river to ride the swells of the oil tankers going by and went under the docks to hunt eels. I say "hunt" because we taped a knife to a broomstick and slashed at the eels as they sunned themselves beneath holes in the docks. They were monster-size eels.

We also hunted rats on the shore. Bill had a shotgun, and we would prowl along the rocky shore next to the drive-in theater. I think the rats came out after all the popcorn spilled on the ground.

Bill was a couple of years older than me, but we were in the same grade. He had been kept back twice. I never understood why. Looking back, I think he probably had an undiagnosed case of dyslexia. He was well behaved, spoke well, and was as knowledgeable as any of us. Our relationship helped me to not judge the capability of others too quickly. This was made very clear to me in an incident we both survived a couple of years later.

Chapter 9

Buy the Beautiful Sea

My mother always talked about having her own summer place by the ocean. She and Joe scouted up and down Rhode Island and southern Massachusetts. She was delighted when they bought a plot of land on Horseneck Beach in Westport, Massachusetts, located between Newport and Cape Cod. Their lot was a climb over the sand dunes to the ocean, and their dock was on the Westport River, only a hundred yards away.

That summer Joe's father came to stay with us to assist in the construction of the cottage. He was a retired carpenter/bricklayer and a World War I infantry veteran. He was very skilled and hardworking. He was a quiet man, except when, in the middle of the night, we could hear him thrashing around in bed, reliving the horrors of combat in the trenches.

Denny and I were conscripted to work with Grampa Collins in the construction of the cinder-block walls of the cottage. Our job was to feed the blocks and mortar mixture to him as he laid the blocks. We worked our asses off trying to keep up with him. The only breaks he took were to roll his own cigarettes. We also dug the hole and trenches for the septic system. This experience convinced me to avidly avoid all future manual labor.

Over that winter, Joe was transferred from the Arnold Hoffman research labs in Providence to their chemical plant in Dighton, Massachusetts, only twenty-five minutes from our new summer home. He landed me a summer job there, where I worked with two college guys. Their constant bantering helped keep our minds off the monotony of our work. We each had a barrel of jade-green dye rolled out to us. We had to scoop the dye out of the barrel and pack it in a small metal box. We then slapped a shipping label on the box, and it was shipped to Karachi, Pakistan. I was told that Pakistanis really liked jade green.

You may have heard of the Blue Man Group; well, we were the Green Men. It took us about thirty minutes to clean up after work.

Summer at the cottage in Westport was a lot of fun. I made friends with a few of the local guys and girls. There were dances every Saturday night at the yacht club on the Westport River. The yacht club was basically a small hall with a luncheon bar, a small beach, and docks. It has been kiddingly referred to as an "Elks Club with Docks."

The local liquor (package) store accepted the phony IDs some of us had. There were two bars on the beach that never checked IDs. Draft beer and shuffleboard are a great combination.

At night we partied in the sand dunes. Six-packs of beer, blankets, and a transistor radio were all we needed. A limbo stick was scavenged up, and everyone tried to see how low they could go.

After a party, I sometimes spent the night in the dunes. I put a blanket down on the highest dune and fell asleep looking at the stars. I rode to work every day with Joe. One morning he came to my room to wake me up and saw an empty bed. He was not amused when I staggered home covered with sand, hungover, and too late for us to make it to work on time. Thankfully, he barely said anything except "hurry."

Chapter 10

Goodbye Saint Paul—Hello La Salle

Don and I were accepted to La Salle Academy for the upcoming sophomore year. La Salle was the Catholic high school for the Providence area and located on the other side of Providence. We regretted the fact that we missed our chance to play football our freshman year because the ninth grade at Saint Paul took the place of a freshman year at high school. However, we found out that we were welcome to show up for spring practice. We raced out of Saint Paul each day to catch a bus downtown and then catch another bus out to La Salle.

On the first day of practice, we were directed by Brother Joseph to the equipment room. He told us to help ourselves. The room was not much bigger than a closet and smelled like year-old sweat and dirty leather. The equipment was all thrown together in a big pile. The pants and jerseys were the opposite of clean, and the helmets and shoulder pads were the source of the dirty-leather smell. We didn't mind; after a while we didn't smell a thing. We participated in most of the spring practices and were told to be sure to come out and join the team in the fall.

Band of Jerks

In June of 1958, I graduated from Saint Paul with honors, despite the fact that I was suspended from school twice. I had been part of a gang of four that clowned around, constantly torturing our rookie teacher. Our classroom was on the third floor. The door to the fire escape was at the front of the room. One day when Sister Mary Joseph left the room, three of us opened the door and went onto the fire escape. We hung a necktie over the railing and when she came back in the room, we carried on like one of us was hanging by his necktie over the railing while the rest of us were struggling to get him back onto the fire escape. She screamed and ran to get help. That was just one of the many stunts we pulled. A year later, I was ridden with guilt to hear the rumor that she had suffered a nervous breakdown.

La Salle was an all-male school taught by the Christian Brothers. One learned quickly that physical punishment was used as a tool to enforce discipline. Brother Anthony was the athletic director. He was a solid six feet, nine inches and rumored to get into the boxing ring with a misbehaving lad and beat the hell out of him. Brother Joseph was the football moderator and mechanical drawing teacher. He was barely over five feet tall, but could do a lot of damage with a T square. He was known as Little Caesar.

My parents were convinced that I was seriously interested in becoming a drummer and found a drum teacher in downtown Providence. My parents had already bought me a used set of drums. Ever since I had banged away on the bass drum in the sixth-grade orchestra, I'd wanted to become a drummer. The drums were set up in our third-floor bedroom, so I was usually able to hammer away on them without annoying anyone. I must have played "Johnny B. Goode" by Chuck Berry a thousand times.

Cement Hands

I made the La Salle football team and started out in junior varsity. I could run like a deer, and at six foot four, I was a perfect profile for the position of end. In those days, playing both offense and defense was common. Blocking and tackling proved to be my strengths—I loved the contact. As a pass receiver, I was adept at getting out in the open but could rarely hang on to the ball. The last time I was thrown to, I was wide open in the end zone and dropped a beautifully thrown pass. Fortunately, my blocking and tackling kept me in the lineup.

Halfway through the season I started practicing with the varsity team and dressed for a couple of games. They put me in the game a few times, usually on defense in desperate goal-line stances.

I made the basketball team, and like football, I started at junior varsity level and was moved up to varsity by the end of the season. Also, like football, I had trouble catching the ball. One time the coach put gloves on me in practice. It had little effect on my case of the "dropsies." I was an excellent rebounder and a strong defender, though. I could drive to the hoop quite well once I caught a pass.

We made it through to the finals. The championship was held at the Providence College Alumni Hall. Mother and Joe were able to make it to the game. I hadn't been in a playoff game so far and didn't expect to play in that one.

I think I chose not to remember who we played against. At halftime we were down by a huge margin. In the middle of the third quarter, the coach sent me in with instructions to "get a damn rebound."

Amazingly enough, I immediately snagged an offensive rebound under the basket and put the ball right back up. I was fouled in the process. During that play, I didn't feel any nervousness. Standing on the foul line, I still didn't feel nervous. I was entitled to two shots because I was fouled in the act of shooting. My first shot made it only two-thirds of the way to the basket. Now I could feel the eyes of 2,600 people—and my mother—all over me and could hear the crowd's murmur of disappointment. At this point I panicked. My second shot didn't even go as far as the first, and the crowd's murmur became a loud rumble, laden with groans.

A guy sitting next to my mother blurted out, "Who the hell is that?"

My mother retorted, "That's my son, so shut your big mouth!"

A Dangerous and Painful Environment

I went out for track that spring. Our coach had no experience in track and field. In fact, I doubt that he knew much about any sport. He just got stuck with the job. I told him I was interested in the high jump and he said that was fine, sounding relieved that he would not have to give any guidance or make a decision.

Practicing the high jump was painful. After you cleared the bar, you landed in a pit filled with very little straw. I incorrectly assumed they would eventually fill up the pit. Today this coach would probably be arrested for child abuse.

Meanwhile, the javelin throwers practiced right next to us. They would throw the javelin back and forth between each other, but not always with the best accuracy. Occasionally, the javelins would land a little too close to the high jump bar. No one ever seemed concerned until one of the javelin guys caught a javelin in the shoulder.

An inept coach, painful landings in a pit with barely any straw, and an environment where a player is run through with a spear was enough for me. I quit.

She's the One

Every Saturday night there was a dance at La Salle's canteen, chaperoned by the Brothers. Couples that danced too closely were admonished to leave room for the Holy Ghost.

Mike O'Rourke lived two streets over from me and was a year ahead of me at La Salle. He drove a beat-up Chevy sedan. Thanks to Mike, I was able to go to the Friday-night La Salle dances throughout the school year.

Sandy, with a big smile and blond hair, danced with me each week. She went to North Providence High School, not far from La Salle. By springtime we were "going steady." We were not able to meet on a regular basis even after school. I was involved with athletics and drum lessons and she was taking piano lessons. I came up with a viable solution to solve the problem of our separation angst, but it became the source of a few difficulties.

Chapter 11

The Red Scooter

*L*ate that spring, Don said he could get us work at a golf course that was being built in Warwick, a city south of Cranston. The only problem was transportation. We were not old enough to get licenses to drive a car, but in Rhode Island you could get a license to drive a motor scooter at the age of fifteen without taking a test.

I saw an ad in the paper for a Cushman motor scooter for $50. I sold my parents on the idea that if they bought the scooter for me, I could pay them back by working on the golf course. I was really excited about having my own transportation so that I would not have to hitchhike to see Sandy in North Providence.

The scooter, 1940s vintage, was bright red and had a seat long enough to hold a passenger. It had a two-speed transmission with a clutch pedal and a brake pedal on the floor, just like a car. The throttle was on the scooter's handlebars. To increase speed, you twisted the throttle up, which is the opposite of a motor-cycle. Top speed was fifty when it was running well. I had not seen anything like it since I lived in Boston, where the ice-cream man came around ringing his bell in a Cushman cart.

We traveled on Route 1 (the Old Post Road) in Warwick to get to the jobsite. There was always a lot of traffic and we drew attention as we putted along. One late afternoon when we were heading home, a car with two morons in it started messing around with us. They were laughing as they cut us off, nearly sending us off the road. Then they would slow down abruptly in front of us. It was all fun and games for them until we came to a red light. Don told me to give him the chain from the bike lock. He ran up to the front of their car and smashed the windshield with the chain. Fortunately, they didn't get out of the car. He jumped back on the scooter and we took off around them when the light turned green. Also, fortunately, they didn't come after us.

Rebels with a Rake

The work on the golf course was akin to being on a chain gang in Mississippi. We shoveled and raked all day under the control of a mean-spirited and cocky straw boss (an informal foreman) who—no surprise—was the son of the contractor. The crew was made up of mostly older guys who seemed to accept being pushed around. I should add that at this point, Don and I had been together through several altercations, usually brought on by his big mouth and my thin skin.

We lasted almost two weeks on the job. Our criticism of the straw boss's leadership skills and our incessant backtalk led him to attack me with a rake. He swiped it across my chest, drawing a little blood; then he turned and ran away. I grabbed a large rock and caught him squarely in the back. He went down hard, then got up and kept running. The crew smiled and shook their heads as the great fighters against tyranny tore off the jobsite on their scooter.

Don and I immediately landed another job we found in an ad. This one was with a storm window and door factory. The company was on the west side of Cranston, so once again, we needed the scooter to get to work.

We lasted a full two weeks in the storm window factory. At first I was a "stringer." I would take the aluminum pieces cut with grooves and thread rubber tubing through them. I was eventually moved up to glass cutting. That was my downfall. I measured wrong and cut a day's worth of production that had to be scrapped. The next day, *I* was scrapped. Don quit shortly after me. I worked the rest of the summer at the Rocky Point Amusement Park in Warwick and ran the "Skill Ball" concession.

Road Trips

In the middle of the summer, Uncle Phil contacted me. He said he was going to be performing in a reenactment of the Lincoln/Douglas debates at a coffeehouse in Hyannis on Cape Cod. At six foot four and an English major at Boston College, Phil was an excellent Abe Lincoln.

Bill Lacasse was always game and agreed to join me on the scooter trip to Hyannis. Traffic was, and is, extremely heavy when getting on and off the Cape on a summer weekend. We had the slowest-moving vehicle on the road. It took us four hours and a lot of harassment to get to Hyannis. Going over the bridges on the Cape Cod Canal was scary, because they rose up sharply high over the canal with low barriers on the sides.

Worse than that—going down the steep hill on President Avenue in Fall River on the way home. I kept my foot on the brake halfway down the hill. Then the brake pedal went all the way down and we started speeding up. I yelled to Bill that the brake had given out. He told me to stop pressing the pedal and wait, and I complied. We kept going faster and only slowed when we went through a cross street.

When we got near the bottom of the street, he told me to press the brake pedal slowly. I did, and it started to slow us down, but not enough to stop us. President Avenue ended at the bottom of the hill, where we had to make a ninety-degree right-hand turn. Luckily, we were able to cut through a gas station on the corner because nobody was at the pumps, and glide to a stop on the side of the cross street.

Bill saved us from a horrible accident because he understood that the scooter had contraction brakes that had become over-heated. He figured that with the engine in high gear, it could not hold us back, and the weight of two large galoots on board didn't help, either. I told him he was as knowledgeable as any of us, and more so in my case.

Love Suppression

My parents were not pleased that Sandy and I were seeing so much of each other. We planned to sneak away and take a trip to the beach. She met me at the top of her street, out of sight of her house, so that her parents wouldn't see her climbing onto the back of an old motor scooter. After we traveled a few miles into Providence, I became concerned that she may be too far back on her seat and could fall off. As usual, I was traveling close to edge of the road so that faster vehicles could pass. I turned my head to look back at her and the next thing I knew the scooter was scraping along the curb of a sidewalk. I jammed on the foot brake and my ankle and the scooter rode along the curb. I managed to get the scooter upright and bring us to a halt.

I had about a six-inch gouge down my leg and ankle. The ankle bone was not damaged, and the wound was not bleeding very much. Like a fool, I persuaded Sandy that I could fix the ankle later. I was not going to let this mishap ruin our day.

Of course, our day was ruined. After a while my ankle started throbbing and then the pain set in. We were in Warwick when I turned us around to head back. She insisted that we go near my house, where she could catch a bus to Providence. From there she could take the bus to La Salle, which continued onto North Providence.

Mother noticed my limp when I entered the house. She examined the wound and recognized that it was several hours old. She was very upset that I had not come home sooner. I think she knew that I had been with Sandy and was probably more upset about that. It was for the best that the scooter's engine finally died.

Chapter 12

Football, Drums, and Deception

*M*y ankle injury healed in time for football season. I played end on offense, but mainly for blocking and very short passes. On defense, I played end and corner linebacker. I loved the physical contact. I believed that, underneath all the football sportsmanship hype, inflicting pain on your opponent is a by-product of good play.

The La Salle football team had a winning history with a Notre Dame–type reputation. By midseason our team, however, was on its way to setting an all-time record for the most losses in school history. I was happy with my performance and did not share the angst and self-flagellation the coaches and most of my teammates were going through. After all, it's only a game. Play hard and have fun has always been my approach to athletics.

My buddy Don had left La Salle and played halfback for Cranston High School. When we played Cranston one Friday-night game, I didn't get a chance to inflict any pain on him. I only remember seeing him smashing through the middle of our defensive line.

We were beaten up so badly that the coach called an early

Saturday-morning practice. He ran us through a new defensive formation. It was called the "Umbrella" defense. That moved me downfield away from the line of scrimmage. I clumsily grabbed a runner in the open field but did not bring him down. A few players piled on and pushed me backward. My ankle went under me and made a loud cracking sound when I hit the ground.

It was the same ankle that had just healed from the scooter accident. I had to stay in bed at home until the swelling subsided in my ankle and the physician could apply the cast. I was also waiting for a condolence visit from one or two of the coaches. That didn't happen. Days later, I received a telephone call from the head coach. He tersely wished me a swift recovery.

The broken ankle didn't heal in time for the basketball season, so that was it for sports that year. However, I was able to continue my drumming lessons, though I was limited to practicing only on the rubber pad, which did not involve any foot movement.

Ricky Rocks

That spring, my drum teacher set me up with a group from the city of East Providence who were forming a band. They came to my house and we set up our equipment in the finished basement. We all blended well, both musically and on a personal level. We agreed to call ourselves the Four Kings. The demographic makeup of our band was almost to a mirror that of Rhode Island's. Our leader was Portuguese and played the accordion. The guitar player was Italian. The sax player was a redhead of English descent, and the drummer was, and still is, Irish. We were only missing a French Canadian.

Our first gigs were Sundays at the East Providence Portuguese and Italian Club. Families gathered for an early dinner, and then all ages took to the dance floor. We had a repertoire of classic standards, rock 'n' roll, and a few ever-popular ethnic tunes like the "Tarantella."

A big move up for us was the Friday-night Sock Hop at a junior high school in East Providence. We were set up on the stage of the auditorium. This was 1959, when rock 'n' roll and Elvis were hitting full stride.

The kids began dancing as soon as we started playing. They applauded loudly after every song. I went into my drum solo in the middle of the set, and everyone began applauding and the girls started screaming like I was Elvis. I couldn't believe this was happening.

When we went on break, I was rushed by a bunch of girls begging me to dance with them. This was the same me that sweated bullets when I asked a girl to dance at the La Salle canteen. I danced a little bit with one girl and then another would cut in, and so it went until the intermission records stopped and we went back onstage. This happened after each set throughout the night. Despite the rocketing increase in my self-esteem, I knew deep down that it was just the times and I was not destined to be a rock star.

Complicit Christina

My mother issued an ultimatum that I was to see Sandy as little as possible. Of course that only hardened my resolve to keep seeing her as much as possible. Sandy's junior prom was coming up and I was sure the family vehicle would not be available to me. Mike was also dating a girl from North Providence. They were going to the prom and invited Sandy and me to ride with them.

I told my parents that my band had a gig requiring a suit and tie. Most of my drum set fit into the trunk of Mike's Chevy; however, the large bass drum did not. Mike and his girlfriend rode in front. Sandy and I were squashed together in the back seat with the big bass drum. This was just one of the many clandestine rendezvous operations we got away with.

Communication was a major problem, though. In those pre–cell phone and personal computer days, the only remote communication device in each household was the telephone. There was only one phone in our house, and it was in a central location with no privacy. My sister Chrissy was a co-conspirator. When Sandy called, she asked to speak to Chrissy and then Chrissy notified me, so I knew to call Sandy back.

That summer, I wanted to avoid another boring manual-labor summer job. I loved the ocean and thought a lifeguard job would be great. Advanced first-aid and senior lifesaving certifications were required. I took the first-aid course at the Cranston YMCA. The fact that mouth-to-mouth resuscitation was part of the protocol led to some amusing teenage banter.

The senior lifesaving training was also at the YMCA. The first night I entered the pool area and was a little intimidated by the large middle-aged guy sitting on a chair at the head of the pool. He had an unlit cigar hanging out of the side of his mouth and barked out commands from a microphone. He was Captain Roger Wheeler, the longtime head of the state lifeguard system. He reminded me of Papa Dobbyn. I passed all the tests.

The two certificates qualified me to become a state non-surf lifeguard, meaning lifeguarding at pools or bayside beaches only. A friend of a friend helped me get a state of Rhode Island lifeguard job. His advice was to go to the office of the State of Rhode Island Parks and Recreation and tell them my state representative sent me.

The office was in the basement of the statehouse. There were a couple of guys waiting outside the office when I got there. They were in and out pretty quickly. I entered the room and told the man at a desk that "so-and-so" sent me and that you might be able to help me get a lifeguard job. He asked me my name and address and I presented my certificates. Although it was a little late to be applying, he thought it was likely I would be hired. The efficiency of a well-oiled patronage system was amazing.

I was assigned a lifeguard position at Goddard Memorial State Park in Warwick. The park is a thick forest with miles of bridle and hiking trails. It has athletic fields, a nine-hole golf course, and a beach on Narragansett Bay. When I worked there, the pavilion housed a carousel. The carousel was built in New York in 1890. It had lived in four amusement parks before being installed in Goddard Memorial State Park in 1931, but was dismantled and sold in 1973. It currently resides in the Jacksonville Zoo in Florida.

The beach was sandy and ran along the edge of the woods. The swimming area was roped off with buoys. Two lifeguards were assigned to work from 10:00 a.m. to 6:00 p.m. each day. My partner, Mary, was a cheerful and athletically built black woman who attended the University of Rhode Island.

Families were attracted to our beach because of the quiet bay water. Navy personnel were frequent visitors because the Quonset Point Naval Air Station and the Naval Construction Training Center for "Sea Bees" were just around the bend.

Once in a great while, we would rush to pick up a toddler who fell down in a foot of water, but we never had occasion to rescue an adult in serious trouble. Our main activity was providing first aid to visitors for cuts caused by stepping on shells or pieces of glass. Explaining to kids that horseshoe crabs did not bite but they should be leery of stepping on their sharp tails helped us pass the time.

Mary and I got along great. She was into sports also, and we were both the eldest of large families and enjoyed trading stories about our growing up. It came up in conversation that we were both born on July fifteenth, and we decided to celebrate together.

I brought a bottle of tawny port wine and she brought a small cake. We agreed that lunchtime was technically off duty and that having a bit of the grape with the cake would be okay.

We had lunch in the carousel pavilion where we could still keep an eye on the beach. We made several trips back to the carousel that afternoon. Feeling very good about everything, we dove into the water for a long swim. We were throwing seaweed at each other as we frolicked our way back to shore, finally getting serious and back to our respective lifeguard stations.

One day, the beach was crowded with an overabundance of Navy guys who were having a jolly good time. State laws forbade the use of alcohol in state parks and on the beaches. However, the prevailing custom has always been somewhat different. You just had to use the proper amount of discretion.

A sailor approached me for help for his bleeding knee. It was obvious he was in violation of the state law governing libations. I called Mary to bring over the first-aid kit and led him off the beach and sat him down on the wall. Mary said she would tape him up. I stood by holding the first-aid box.

When she started cleaning the wound, he started pawing at

her hair. She instantly told him to stop it. He did it again. She said that if he did it again, she would cut his other knee.

He did it again and she jabbed his good knee with the scissors. After a short expletive, he shut up and she proceeded to bandage up both knees.

Mary and I would occasionally grab a bite to eat after work. I could sense all the eyes on our backs as we entered the restaurants. Biracial couples drew a lot of attention back then. I mistakenly believed that in the future, mixed-race couples would draw very little, if any, attention.

Chapter 13

A Turbulent Transition

*J*ust before I started my senior year, I broke my wrist playing touch football on Horseneck Beach. The Four Kings were going in a different direction, so my rock star days were over. My parents gave up trying to separate Sandy and me. Maybe they realized what I came to believe later in life: that the more they tried to break us up, the more our defiance brought us closer together.

By the time my wrist healed well enough to play, the basketball season was well underway. The starting five looked solid without me; and I was not willing to sit on the bench, hoping to work my way up to getting a lot of playing time.

Other than young Brother Peters whacking me on the head from behind with a heavy physics book for not paying attention, my studies were going well. I was getting above-average grades in most subjects.

Throughout high school, every person I met assumed my nickname was Dick. My father had been called Dick, so to avoid confusion my family called me Ricky and friends called me Rick. I tired of correcting everyone, and since confusion in the family was no longer a problem, I morphed into Dick. The problem I created is when non-family members mix socially or just hear about me, they wondered who this Rick was.

Rookie Coaches

Frank Busher was a friend of mine from La Salle, CYO basketball, and pickup games. CYO players were ten to thirteen years old. We volunteered to coach the Saint Michaels CYO team that my brother Denny played on. He was fast and good on defense. We had a couple of pretty good shooters, but no real stars. Our strength was outrunning the other team and playing a very physical game.

Saint Patrick's usually won the Greater Providence CYO league championship and had a well-seasoned coach. Much to our amazement, we made the finals of the playoffs and faced Saint Patrick's in a best two-out-of-three series. They had a fantastic shooter and demolished us in the first game. In the second game, we sent in Bobby to guard their superstar. Bobby was a big kid and an excellent athlete, but he had never played basketball. His instructions were to harass his man and not worry about fouling out. Bobby did a great job. The shooter totally lost his cool and was thrown out of the game. We went on to win. They caught on to our strategy in the third game and demolished us once again.

Denny attended La Salle but chose not to play athletics there. During freshman initiation week at Siena College, upperclassmen on the lacrosse team, as part of the hazing, forced him to play goalie while they all took shots at him. He had never played lacrosse, but defended so well they suggested he try out for the team. He made the team. In his senior year he was Siena's MVP and had the most saves of any goalie in the country.

After college, Denny returned to La Salle and started up a lacrosse program, which eventually led them to a Rhode Island state title. He and some friends founded Tannerhill, a group home for children. He later taught history at Moses Brown in Providence and continued to play in leagues. He coached a club lacrosse team at Roger Williams College and made it into a varsity sport. In 2002 he was on the US Senior Lacrosse team that won world title in Perth, Australia. He is in the New England and Rhode Island Halls of Fame.

Denny enjoys telling everyone how, in grammar school, I paid him to fight kids that gave me a tough time. If I fought a kid three years younger than me, it would have made me a bully. I always tell him I did it to toughen him up and that helped him to become such a tough competitor in lacrosse. Yeah, right.

My Guidance Counselor

I was very anxious to get to college, away from parental supervision and the daily family squabbles about whose turn it was to do the dishes or who was taking forever to get out of the bathroom in the morning rush. My applications to Boston College and Holy Cross were both accepted.

My mother provided some wise options as to which one I should attend. She knew I was rebellious and not very good at taking orders. In light of the military draft that was in place, she feared that as an enlisted man, I would end up being court-martialed. She cautioned me to avoid the Army and join the Navy, where you almost always had hot food and a bed. Holy

Cross had a Navy ROTC program; however, she also said that with a liberal arts degree, I would end up selling frozen orange juice to supermarkets. Boston College had a business school, but the ROTC program was Army. I chose BC.

My grades and college entrance tests were good enough to qualify for a state of Rhode Island scholarship. As the eldest of nine, I felt obligated to earn as much as I could to pay my own way through college. The scholarship and stipend earned from ROTC contributed toward that goal.

Where Is Everybody?

I was very pleased to be notified by the state that I had a lifeguard job for the summer. I had passed the surf lifeguard test and was looking forward to working at a major saltwater beach. Instead, I was assigned to Randall Pond, located in the middle of the city of Cranston.

I had never heard of this body of water in my own city. The reason: nobody went there. It was a small pond in the mostly industrial section of town. There was no lifeguard chair, or a lifesaving buoy, or a first-aid kit. I had to lifeguard from a weedy dirt clearing on the shore. My guess was that maybe someone had drowned there and the public pressed the state for a lifeguard.

It was a short hitchhike to commute to the pond. My family had moved to the beach for the summer, so I had the house to myself.

Every day at work, I built a small fire and cooked two hot dogs for lunch. I never saw anyone enter the water for a swim. My only company was a few neighborhood kids and a gay guy that was always flirting with me.

As the summer wore on, I started arriving late and leaving early. During the last couple of weeks, I didn't show up at all.

One early evening I got a phone call from someone who sounded like a friend of mine. He asked, "How are things going at Randall Pond?"

Laughingly, I replied, "How the hell should I know? I haven't been there lately."

My supervisor angrily responded, "You no longer are or ever will be employed by the state of Rhode Island!" I was embarrassed to be caught like that, but had no intentions to run for office.

Overrun

Sandy's father was in Our Lady of Fatima Hospital with a staph infection that summer, and passed away that September. She had to deal with the grief of losing her father, who was only forty-eight years old, and the stress of enrolling in college. Rhode Island College is in Providence, only a few miles from her home, so least she was able to be with her mother.

In September 1961, the annual Greater Providence Football Round Robin was held on the Friday night before my enrollment day at Boston College. Don and I attended as alumni of Cranston High and La Salle Academy. We finished a pint of whiskey in the stands and then decided to wander around the stadium. We ran into many fellow players and rivals.

"Hey, Chowderhead," someone yelled from the stands as we walked by. Don hated that moniker.

Don yelled back, "Come on down here and say that!" The mouthy guy was from Warwick, which was a big rival of Cranston. He looked around at the head-nodding of his contingent and it became obvious that they were all coming down to see us.

Don nailed the "big mouth" with a sucker shot to the jaw as soon as he approached. Then we came under a full attack from his gang. During the battle, I kept seeing Don pop up, slug someone, and then disappear only to reemerge and clock someone else. I was taking shots to the head and failed to land a good punch. Next thing I knew, four guys grabbed me by the arms and legs and threw me over the railing onto the football field several feet below. For a second it looked like they were going to jump onto the field to continue beating the hell out of me.

While I lay on the ground, I noticed that they were starting to get the hell beat out of them. Our friends from the Providence Central High football alumni rescued us. We were friends with their quarterback and had played a lot of playground basketball with his teammates. Don suffered very little damage, but my entire face was swollen and covered with large bumps.

The following Monday I enrolled in Boston College. I kept the photo ID taken that day in my wallet for many years, to remind myself what a combative clown I could be.

Chapter 14

Work, Play, and Study

*T*o my surprise, at college I was assigned to the business school honors program. This was a mistake on their part: I'd hit a wall in calculus, which was only required in the honors program. I had earned above-average grades in high school math, mostly by memorizing formulas rather than by understanding the concepts.

The calculus professor, with his wild white hair, actually looked like a mad scientist. He wrote formulas on the blackboard with his right hand, which he erased with his left. That really didn't matter to me, because I hadn't the slightest idea what calculus was about. I was relieved to find out that because I did not elect the honors courses, I received credit but was taken out of the honors program.

I had an excellent basic accounting teacher that year. He instructed us that "accounting is the language of business." Accounting uses only basic math and has a logic that is different from higher math. I grasped that logic and ended up selecting accounting as my major.

Money was really tight for me that year, partly because of my trips downtown to the jazz clubs. Two of my dorm-mates were also cash poor. Since most of our fellow students complained about the cafeteria food, we figured that a tasty supplement would sell. We borrowed money to buy and sell sandwiches throughout the dormitories. We bought dozens of roast beef sandwiches on bulky rolls with Russian dressing from the famous Elsie's in Harvard Square.

One night I had a bag full of sandwiches and knocked on the first door in the dorm. I was horrified to be greeted by a student holding a slice of pizza.

Unbeknownst to us, someone else had entered the business and already sold through the dorms. We couldn't unload our inventory. Since we were operating entirely on borrowed capital, we took a big hit and had to go out of business.

Mea Culpa, Mea Culpa, Mea Maxi Culpa

The three of us had a brainstorming session in my dorm room about how to get some quick cash. The moral turpitude of what we planned to do greatly surpassed my earlier shoplifting days. We decided to hold a raffle that nobody could win except us. The fictional first prize was a color television and the equally fictional second was $500 cash.

Tickets were fifty cents each and three for a dollar. Our spiel was that we were from a fraternity, Omicron Nu Epsilon, and were raising money for a scholarship fund. We did not realize that Omicron Nu Epsilon was actually a sorority!

We scraped together only enough money to have five hundred tickets printed and gave the printer a phony name and address, telling him we would be back to buy more.

With the freshly printed tickets in hand, we took the trolley that ran from BC to downtown Boston and got off at each stop to sell a few tickets and then moved on down the line. Early in this scam, I knocked on an apartment door and a young woman answered. I gave her my pitch and she asked me to just wait a minute. She returned with her son's piggy bank and shook out a dollar. This made me feel lower than whale shit. My friends felt just as guilty and we ceased operations that first day.

So then I went legit and bagged groceries and stocked shelves at the Stop & Shop supermarket near BC. Christmas vacations I worked as an elf with Santa Claus and wrapped gifts at the Outlet Department Store in Providence.

I often hitchhiked home with a bag of dirty laundry. One Sunday afternoon, I was heading back to school and was hitchhiking on South Main Street in Providence. A reporter from the *Providence Journal* interviewed me and took my picture. I had forgotten about it until my next dirty-laundry visit home. My mother proudly showed me the article on hitchhiking that she had cut out of the paper. It included a picture of me wearing my Australian wool bush hat and standing in the snow with my thumb out.

The Army ROTC program not only helped with my college tuition, but it also offered me a chance to postpone getting a real job after graduating. I envisioned spending a couple of years seeing the world as an Army officer and then becoming a big-time business manager. We were not at war, so what could go wrong?

The first couple of years in ROTC, all I remember doing was marching around the parking lot and getting yelled at for not shining my shoes. In ROTC, like the real Army, you could move up in rank. I was never promoted past private. There was a group of us who were relegated to what became known as the Goon Platoon. We proudly wore our single-stripe private rank for four years, rarely polished our brass insignia and, to a man, could not understand what marching in step in neatly pressed pants and shiny shoes had to do with leading men in combat.

I landed a job in my sophomore year with BC's nursing school. I had to sweep the staircases one afternoon per week. I felt like a chump doing this in front of all the young ladies. Early Saturday morning, I had to clean the school's cafeteria floor. Dealing with the buffing machine early in the morning while suffering from a hangover was a bitch. The money earned, though, was applied to my room and board.

That year Sandy's mother married Herman and moved in with him in Croton Falls, New York. Sandy moved into the dorms. Seeing each other in the summer became much more difficult.

A Human Lab Rat

Harvard Medical School ran an ad in the paper for a person to take part in a six-week research project. They were trying to determine how effectively the mind worked under stress. I signed up.

Stress was created by electric shock to my ankle while I sat in a chair with a light in front of me and a box overhead that made a swishing-like sound. I was hooked up to several monitors. The technicians would continuously run different sequences of light, sound, and shock. For example: light-sound-light-sound-light-sound-shock!

The first day I just sat there. Each of the remaining four or five sessions I was given tests periodically requiring mental effort on my part. My favorite test was how long I could recall the different sequences I had gone through. All in all, it was an informative experience and a bit of fun.

On a visit home I learned that my parents were having a house built in Bristol, Rhode Island, which was a suburb on the east side of Narragansett Bay. Totally wrapped up in my own interests, I'd failed to listen carefully about the timing of their move. As a result, on my next three-hour hitchhike home, I discovered that my house was locked and empty. It was another two hours thumbing home to Bristol on the other side of the Bay. I know what you are thinking, but I am not stealing a line from Rodney "I get no respect" Dangerfield. This really did happen.

My junior year driving a taxi for Red Cab was quite profitable. There was a lot of flexibility in that I had to work only a minimum of four hours on a weekday and four on the weekend. I could pick up a cab whenever one was available. My roommate and I would fill in for each other to meet the minimum requirements.

On my first day, I started off parked at a hotel taxi stand. A man got into the cab and asked me to take him to the airport. When he saw me open up a map, he swore and jumped out of the cab.

Boston streets were, and still are, very confusing. Even with a good sense of direction, I sometimes became lost and had to call the dispatcher for help. I was ripped off twice by armed passengers who insisted on a free ride, but at least they didn't knife, shoot, or rob me.

One afternoon, an elderly woman exclaimed that she was having a heart attack. She wanted me to take her directly to her doctor's office, and gave me the address. I called the dispatcher for directions and he arranged a rendezvous with the police, who escorted me to the doctor's office. In my panicked state, I neglected to shut off the meter. At the end of my shift, I got in an argument with the station manager (who was an exact copy of Danny DeVito in *Taxi* in all respects, except he was nastier). I ended up having to pay Red Cab for all the mileage to the doctor's office.

Not all of my cab-driving experiences were negative. I met a lot of pleasant, interesting people, and some were very generous. One elderly woman was a regular rider every week, and either my roommate or I would try to be there for her. She lectured us on the value of staying in college and gave us a $10 tip on a $5 fare.

Out of the blue, Papa Dobbyn called to say that every Thursday he took one of my aunts and uncles to dinner, and I was welcome to join them anytime. All I had to do was let him know that day. They always went to the Lafayette House, located south of Boston, in Foxborough.

A month or so later I called him up and arranged to meet him at his house, which was only a couple of miles from BC. The food at Lafayette House was fantastic. I usually ordered the junior filet mignon with Delmonico potatoes and baked Alaska for dessert.

Meeting Papa at his house gave us the opportunity to have in-depth conversations while we waited for the others to arrive. He was the treasurer for both Jack and Ted Kennedy's senate campaigns. During my senior year he told me that, as the treasurer of the Kennedy campaigns, he was under investigation for violation of election laws.

Even though he had a cadre of Kennedy lawyers, he was very concerned. He said an investigative reporter from the *New York Herald* initiated the action. He kept me abreast of his case whenever we met. The investigation died out, mainly because the *Herald* went out of business.

During that time, Papa was admitted to the hospital with emphysema.

When I went to visit him, I found him sitting up in bed, smoking a cigarette and surrounded by paperwork. (He got out of bed and crossed the room to his oxygen bottle. I thought we were going to blow up.) He told me he was working on the plans for the John F. Kennedy Presidential Library. I visited the library recently and discovered he was listed as a trustee.

The Franklin Sisters

My roommate and I signed up with the BC radio station to do a jazz show. We did a weekly show for a couple of months. The biggest problem we had was complying with the sign on the wall behind the microphone, which instructed DO NOT SAY "AND NOW" OR "NEXT." You may think it sounds easy, but it isn't. To this day, I marvel at the many different phrases DJs use to introduce the next song.

We had a decent collection of albums available to us and we had similar tastes. We both loved the blues. One of us was always sifting through the albums for new songs when we were in the studio.

One of us picked an album of gospel songs sung by Erma Franklin, Aretha's older sister. Later we came across a gospel album *Songs of Faith*, sung by Aretha. We played cuts off both albums all the time. This was 1963. Aretha didn't make it big until 1967. We took great pride and, on occasion, boasted that we discovered one of the greatest modern singers of all time—a bit of hubris, to say the least.

Chapter 15

Cape Cod National Seashore

Joe McLanaghan, a friend from La Salle who went to Providence College, contacted me about a lifeguard job. He told me that the National Park Service was looking for lifeguards for the newly created Cape Cod National Seashore. The interviews were being held in Wellfleet at the beginning of May.

Joe and I hitchhiked to Wellfleet and were interviewed by a "Smokey the Bear" park ranger in one of the Army barracks in the abandoned Camp Wellfleet. He told us the only federal lifeguards were at Cape Hatteras on the Outer Banks. He didn't know a lot about being a lifeguard, and it was apparent that they did not have much time to staff up for the opening of the beaches.

We presented our Rhode Island surf lifeguard certificates and filled out applications. We were hired on the spot, subject to successful completion of the in-the-water test. The test was scheduled for the next week and was to be held in Provincetown. They promised us accommodations in the barracks.

A week later, we hitchhiked back to Wellfleet from Providence and arrived late in the afternoon. A ranger led us to the barracks, furnished with basic Army cots.

At ten in the morning, we were all lined up along Herring Cove Beach at the tip of the Cape in Provincetown. The guy next to me had mentioned that he lived in Provincetown. I asked him why he was covering his body with Vaseline. He said, "You'll find out."

I knew that the water temperature in Rhode Island and southern Massachusetts beaches in the middle of May was a little nippy. Except for surfers in wet suits, most people waited until June to enter the water. Still, I thought that the guy covered in grease was being a bit of a wimp. Just putting one foot in the water, however, changed my mind.

I was totally ignorant of the effect the warm water of the Gulf Stream had on the New England coastal water temperatures. The Gulf Stream travels along the East Coast and bounces off the part of Cape Cod that faces south, where it warms the beach water. Horseneck Beach is one of the beaches that reaps that benefit. The Gulf Stream misses the eastern side of the Outer Cape and does not hit land again until the southern coast of Nova Scotia.

We were in and out of the numbing water for several hours. Every time I went in, I yelled like a kung fu expert breaking a brick in half, except it was in pain.

That night we had dinner in a pizza joint in Wellfleet. I was still shivering so badly I needed two hands to drink my beer. I shivered until I fell asleep in my Army cot.

Joe and I were assigned to Coast Guard Beach in Eastham. It had been an active Coast Guard station until 1958 and was one of nine lifesaving stations that had existed along the Outer Cape starting in 1860.

We met our fellow lifeguards for the beach—Bill and Bob. We went in together to rent a cabin. It was only about a mile or so from the beach. That was the good thing. The bad thing was that it was a tiny little cabin.

Our landlady, Christine Young, lived across the street in a two-story, classic Cape with gray shingles right on Depot Pond. Christine, a widow in her midfifties, was quite vibrant and young in spirit. She welcomed us warmly and encouraged us to drop by for a coffee and a chat, which we often did. She was very proud of her son, David, an artist in New York City.

During the first three weeks on the job, we had to survive without a paycheck. We pooled our meager funds and created an expenditure survival plan. We allocated our funds between sausage, pasta, and Ballantine beer. Bob was from the Portuguese community in Fall River and was able to get a deal on a three-week supply of chorizo sausage. The market and liquor store nearby had a summer sale on cases of Ballantine beer, which was cheaper than buying water. After we started receiving our paychecks, we didn't eat sausage or pasta again that summer, but we never stopped drinking Ballantine.

Bill was the "old man" of the group. His nickname was Chubbs. He started college late and was going into his senior year. He was selected as captain of the six-man crew at Coast Guard Beach. The chief ranger had no experience with lifeguarding and relied on Chubbs to help him develop operating rules and procedures. Chubbs sold the idea that chatting up young ladies was goodwill for the National Park Service and should be encouraged.

The sandbars along the Outer Cape beaches were the cause of many strong riptides. The waves would break over the bars and then run back out between them. Most of our rescues were plucking people out of the rips as they were being swept out to sea. When the surf was big, we would stand on the shore with buoy in hand and prevent people from swimming where we knew the rip was.

Many of the folks that visited our beach had never been to the ocean before. It was not uncommon for someone to ask, "Where does the tide go when it goes out?" We couldn't resist saying England.

We had balsa-wood buoys painted red and gray, and they looked like a double-ended torpedo or artillery shell. A rope line was passed through a hole and tied off on one end of the buoy. We planted the buoys in the sand and draped the line on top of the buoy so that we could grab it on the run to rescue someone. The most common question, most always asked by a man, was, "So what do you do with those things? Shoot them out to save someone?" Joe and I talked about how often we were asked that question and how we might have some fun.

The next person who asked me if we shot the buoys out, I responded, "Yes, sir, we do. Would you like a demonstration?" He said he would. I stood up on the lifeguard chair and whistled over to Joe, gesturing to the buoy. People got wind of what was happening and started gathering around the buoy. As planned, Joe came running over with a first-aid box. I took the line off the buoy and laid it straight out behind the buoy. He opened the box and handed me a pack of matches.

The excitement grew when I warned everyone to step back away from the buoy. I lit a match and tried to light the end of the rope. I did this several times and then with a laugh, confessed that we did not shoot it out.

Remarkably enough, everyone seemed to get a kick out of it, including the victim who asked the question. I explained that we attached the buoy with the line to our person when we went into the water. I think that some of the older people who asked that question may have assumed they knew the answer, because buoys actually were shot out in the early days.

We Told You So!

We trained every morning. One guard stayed on the beach and the rest swam two hundred yards. One morning, I was about fifty yards behind the others. Suddenly the guard on the beach started blowing his whistle and was waving frantically for us to come in. The guys in front of me turned and swam rapidly back to the beach.

Then I heard him yell, "Shark! Shark! Get out!" I thought he was joking until the large fin crossed about twenty feet in front of me. I remembered that you shouldn't splash around, giving the appearance of a wounded fish or a distressed mammal. So I used a breaststroke with a frog kick to glide my way toward shore.

It was just our luck that it was one of the hottest days of the summer and the beach was jammed. We told everyone about the shark and announced that swimming was canceled. People were outraged. They kept coming up to each of us to express their frustration, often quite vehemently.

The beach had sandbars offshore and, as the tide went out, one could swim to the sandbar and then stand up. Chubb decided that if each of us stood on a sandbar, we could keep watch. We headed out to the sandbars with our buoys and allowed the crowd on the beach to go into the water behind the sandbars.

The Gulf Stream had been pushed offshore, so the water temperature was in the fifties. My teeth were starting to chatter when a roar went up from the beach. A shark fin had appeared.

The shark was cruising along the beach just outside the sandbars.

No need to blow our whistles. Everyone was already scrambling out of the water. On our way back to the beach, we helped ashore those who were moving too slowly.

As I was drying off, several people came up to me and expressed their apologies for the complaining they had done. That was quite satisfying. We did not see the shark again that day.

We got word the next day that a Coast Guard helicopter had shot a twelve-foot great white along the beach farther north of us. It was shot because its behavior indicated a sickness and an inability to feed normally. From what I have read, great whites do not prey on humans. They will sometimes mistake a surfer or a swimmer for a seal, and they do hold the world record for the most bites each year.

Currently, seals are now abundant in the summer along the Outer Cape beaches. In my time, we saw only a few, if any, and then only in September. I recently returned to Coast Guard and Nauset Light Beaches, just for old times' sake. I was shocked to see that there were signs warning everyone to stay out of the water if seals were nearby, because the great whites were in the vicinity in search of their favorite meal.

David X. Young

At night, and on our days off, we all worked in the food business. We washed dishes, bused tables, shoveled ice cream, grilled hamburgers, and fried clams. I used this money to pay my summer living expenses and banked the lifeguard pay for college.

My hangout after work was the Land Ho! in Orleans. Orleans

is the town just before you get to Eastham and the National Seashore. The Land Ho! is a bar and restaurant in the center of town. It was there that I met our landlady Christine's son, David, the artist. In the summer his studio was the loft over the Land Ho!, and the rest of the year he lived in New York.

His studio in Manhattan was a large loft on Canal Street in the flower district. He was well known in the art community and maintained friendships with Jackson Pollock, Willem de Kooning, Franz Kline, and the actor Zero Mostel. He loved jazz and his loft was at the center of the jazz scene in the city. He would regularly host jam sessions, often extending into the wee hours of the morning. Thelonious Monk, Pee Wee Russell, Zoot Sims, and Charles Mingus were regulars.

David mentioned that he shared the loft with photojournalist W. Eugene Smith. From 1957 to 1965 Smith was working on his "Jazz Loft Project." He photographed and recorded the jazz musicians that flowed in and out of the loft. In his early years he photographed extensively in the front lines of World War II, in the Pacific theater.

"Thumbing" to New York

I managed to squeeze in two visits to Sandy that summer, where she was staying with her mother and Herman and working a summer job with *Reader's Digest*. I hitchhiked to White Plains and took a train to Croton Falls. Luckily, every ride I got was timely and with a friendly driver, except for the fellow who was so intoxicated he was scaring me to death by swerving all over the road. I demanded he stop and let me out of the car, which he did.

On one of my visits, Herman took us out to the local German Club. We had an enjoyable evening with steins of beer and singing and dancing to the oompah band.

The rest of the summer continued to be great fun. I managed to party hearty despite working two jobs.

Chapter 16

Let the Good Times Roll!

*T*he second summer, the four of us lifeguards moved to a house the National Park had purchased for eventual demolition. It was called the Dowdy House and was built in the Civil War era. It was a mile from the ocean and rent-free; we only had to pay the utilities.

Chubbs and I had been reassigned to Nauset Light Beach. It is just a mile up the coast from Coast Guard Beach. Starting in Eastham, a cliff runs along a large part of the twenty miles of beach on the Outer Cape. The old lighthouse stood on the cliff next to a small parking lot. Access to the beach was via a very long set of stairs. It required only three guards.

It seemed like every night whoever was home would end up hosting an impromptu party. The Dowdy House became known as the "Lifeguard House" and was party central. Sometimes things would get out of hand. One night the house was jammed and when I looked around, I didn't see anyone I knew. Things started to get ugly as a couple of strangers were getting on my case. One guy with a big mouth seemed to have it in for me.

My friend Frank and a couple of other South Providence boys

had restaurant jobs in nearby Chatham and had been night surf fishing. Frank came in the door holding up a large pollock. "Hey, Dobbyn, look what I caught."

Coincidently, the mouthy guy started to launch an attack on me. One of Frank's guys quickly intervened with a knife and cut him enough to make him run out the door. The house emptied rapidly. I was reminded of the time my butt was saved by my Providence basketball friends at the round-robin football game.

Drummer Boy Meets Jazz Men

The Land Ho! had booked a jazz duet for after-dinner entertainment. Dick Wetmore, "Dickie," played the cornet and the violin. The Village Gate house piano player was the other half of the duet.

One evening David Young and I were having a few drinks and listening to them play when he said, "Didn't you say you played the drums?" I told him that I'd played in a rock 'n' roll band in high school. He pointed out that someone had left a floor tom-tom in the corner. I went over and pulled it back to our table and then played along a little with the duo.

Dickie sat down with us after the set and asked if I was interested in playing with the them. Without hesitation, I said, "Absolutely."

The following night, Dickie told me the owner would pay me ten dollars a night, a free dinner (except steak or lobster), and free beer. Such a deal! I was in!

I retrieved my drums from home, and on my days off I started playing with the "trio." We played popular standards, blues, and classical jazz. Dick broke me in by insisting that my only job was to lay down a simple beat. Nothing fancy was required. They let me know the instant I got ahead or behind the beat.

David told me that Dickie had played the electric violin in Woody Herman's band. I later learned that he had been a sideman, playing trumpet and violin for many of the jazz greats of the time. The piano player never said much. I think they both viewed the gig as a paid vacation.

The Orleans Inn down the street booked jazz and folk entertainers. It was very common for some of these musicians to drop by the Land Ho! and sit in with Dickie's trio. Some of the pop-in visitors were on vacation and came just to see him and to jam a little.

One Sunday night, Zoot Sims showed up with his sax. He was joined by a couple of his friends with a trumpet and a trombone. We played mostly Dixieland, which favored my ability to not screw up too much. To this day, I have trouble believing that I was afforded the opportunity to play with some of the best jazz talent of that era.

Quite often, Dave would invite a bunch of us up to his loft after the Land Ho! closed. The beer was always flowing and we generally danced our asses off. He had a collection of current rock records. Everyone's favorite was the frenetic, "Do You Love Me" by the Contours.

Hitting the water the morning after at 0900 for the mandatory training swim was tough. Even tougher was staying awake and vigilant in the lifeguard chair all day. On a day when I was really exhausted and the surf was calm, I would get the okay to take a mile run down to Coast Guard Beach. I ran just enough to get out of sight and then took a power nap.

Luckily, the lifeguard rescue work had been light, mostly

entailing pulling kids out of the surf or helping adults who had been tumbled by a breaker and could not regain a footing. One fellow had a heart attack, and I got a real workout racing down the beach and up the stairs to the phone booth. I was huffing and puffing so much I had trouble speaking to hit up a visitor for a dime to call the rescue squad.

Crunch Time

It was two weeks before Labor Day, the beach was very crowded, and the surf was big. I don't remember why, but we were short one guard that day, so it was just Captain Chubbs and me.

Chubbs started blowing his whistle at two boys and a girl who were swimming into one of the riptides near his station, but it was too late! They couldn't turn back, and all three of them were rapidly heading out to sea.

I jumped up off my stand, grabbed my torpedo buoy, and raced down the beach. Chubbs headed into the water with the rescue surfboard. I reached his stand, picked up the reel of "surf line," and attached the torpedo to the line. I ran to the spot where he had launched the surfboard.

We had been instructed only verbally on how to rescue with the surf line and had not had any practice drills. One guard was to work the reel from the beach, and the other would swim out with the buoy that was attached to the line. The problem was there was not a guard available to stay on the beach.

A small crowd had gathered around me. Several men eagerly offered to help. I quickly told them that when I waved my arm back and forth, they could start bringing the line in. I said whatever you do, do it slowly! I explained that the best way to do that was "for all of you to hold on to the line and slowly walk back up the beach while pulling. If you ran out of beach and needed more room, the last man could peel off and go to the head of the line," and so on.

I swam out using a breaststroke so I could keep my eyes on where Chubbs was. It was slower than freestyle but was more powerful. I needed the power to bust through the waves with the buoys and to handle the increasing weight of the length of the line.

When I reached Chubbs, I saw that he had the young lady on the board with him and the two boys were hanging on the edge of the board. He said, "What took you so long?"

I was so out of breath I could barely speak. I was thinking, *Screw you*, but I said, "That line is really heavy!"

I wrapped the loose torpedo around the reel line and kept its line connected to me. I then instructed each guy to hang on to a torpedo. I positioned myself behind them and put a hand on their backs. Chubbs saw I had it set up and paddled off to the beach.

I said, "Hang on tight, boys," and then waved my arm back and forth. We started moving along nicely at first.

Then they started pulling too hard and we picked up speed to a point where I was going underwater. My passengers were able to keep their heads up and breathe, but I had to fight hard to reach the top of the water. I couldn't stay up, so I held my breath for a while and then came up again.

The problem was I had already been breathing heavily when we started, so I could not keep this going very long. Another problem was that I had not thought to come up with a slow-down signal. Yelling "SLOW DOWN" was not working either. They had obviously forgotten the part about pulling slowly.

They got an A for effort, though, because we started moving even faster. I knew I was going to drown if I stayed connected to the surf line and the buoys.

It was a major struggle to get the buoy line off me. I almost reached the point of swallowing sea water. I finally broke free and burst to the top of the water, gasping for air. What a relief it was to see the two boys still on top of the water, gliding through the waves to the beach.

I didn't have any strength left. I just floated on my back outside the breakers for a long time and then worked my way to the beach.

Chubbs and I received rather blasé expressions of gratitude from the three teenage clowns we saved. We didn't even get to say "just doin' our jobs."

Very Bad Behavior

Several days later, Chubbs and I had a falling out. Every Labor Day, Orleans had a parade. It was not officially sanctioned and did not include the usual fire trucks, "dignitaries" in convertibles, and a high school band.

Instead, year-round bar regulars and temporary summer workers were the main participants. Crazy costumes with a nautical theme were prevalent. There was a Mardi Gras atmosphere, and I had signed up with Dick Wetmore and Co. to play a snare drum in the back of a truck.

Chubbs said there was no way he would or could get me Labor Day off. We argued vehemently for days. My (weak) position was that there were guards available from one of the bigger beaches who could fill in for me. I was being a real jerk and was basically guilty of dereliction of duty. In the end, I selfishly played my little snare drum in the Labor Day parade. At that time, I justified my behavior by telling myself that it was the last summer I would be "free." Chubbs and I barely spoke before we departed. To this day I am totally ashamed of my behavior.

Joe and I hitchhiked backed home together from the Cape. We stopped in Fall River for lunch and a beer at the Portuguese and Italian Club. We left about four in the afternoon. My roommate Jim from New York had offered to meet me at my house and give me a ride to BC. I staggered into the house at dinnertime. He had been waiting for me at least a couple of hours. My mother was so upset she threw my dinner at me, plate and all. Jim hustled me out of the house and got me up to Boston.

A month later I received a letter of commendation from the National Park Service for my performance in the successful multiperson rescue at Nauset Light Beach.

A month after that, I received a letter informing me that I would never be able to work for the National Park Service again.

Chapter 17

Life Speeds Up

*F*our of us rented an apartment off-campus for our senior year: my dorm roommate, Jim; my accounting-major friend Paul Arnold Pellini, alias Pap; Paul's friend Bill, from Fitchburg, Massachusetts, and me. Bill, like me, had a longtime girlfriend back home.

Our place was a great location in the Allston section of Boston. Not too far a commute, and bars and restaurants were plentiful. It was only a two-minute walk to a workingman's bar that claimed to be one of the longest bars in Boston. It could also have been the narrowest. The bar, with stools, ran the length of the building, and a shelf on the wall ran parallel for standing customers. They were open all day and into the night, starting first thing in the morning. The menu was limited to pickled eggs, pickled sausage, pretzels, and potato chips. A shot and a beer were the favored libation.

This was our watering hole, and the bartender had adopted us somewhat. After two drinks he would start nagging us to leave and go home to study. When we graduated, we thanked him for all the times he nagged us.

Sandy had bought a used VW Bug, and we were able to spend weekends together in the apartment. I had managed to save a lot from my summer work, so we could dine out at a real restaurant occasionally. We found a small Italian restaurant, where we ordered a bottle of Chianti with dinner. I had never before ordered anything but beer with a meal. These were good times. We planned to get married in August.

I had gained a firm grasp on the concepts of accounting and finance and was actually enjoying those advanced classes. Whenever possible, I took elective courses outside of the Business School. I took several psychology courses in the Liberal Arts School. I even had a poem published in the quarterly literary magazine. I graduated with a major in accounting and a minor in psychology.

I had to choose which branch of the Army I preferred to serve in. I had to submit three choices. The catch was one of them had to be a combat arm. Mother's advice rang in my ears. "Stay the hell out of the infantry and anything to do with tanks or big guns. Join the Quartermaster Corp, like your father."

The combat arms were Infantry, Armor, Artillery, and Military Police. In order, I chose the Quartermaster Corps, Army Intelligence, and the Military Police. I got the Military Police.

Oops

In March, we found out that Sandy was pregnant and the baby was due in October. Sandy consulted with her obstetrician regarding the feasibility of an August wedding. He said that she would not be "showing" too much if she watched her weight and wore a girdle under the wedding dress.

My mother took me shopping at a large discount store for

an engagement ring. It was not a big surprise to Sandy when I knelt down and presented the ring to her. It was official: we were engaged.

Sandy's stepfather, Herman, passed away that spring. Her mother moved back to North Providence to live with her own stepfather. He was a builder from Germany and had built his own house and the house across the street, which Sandy had grown up in.

Daily Push-Ups

After graduation, I reported to Fort Devens for ROTC officer boot camp. Fort Devens was thirty miles west of Boston. The training lasted six weeks, and upon successful completion, one became a commissioned officer with the rank of second lieutenant.

We had the stereotypical kick-ass drill sergeant. He significantly broadened my knowledge of racy epithets and idioms. "If you are looking for sympathy, look in the dictionary between shit and syphilis" was one of his favorites.

He took a perverse interest in me and a couple of wiseasses from New York. I think we did more push-ups than the rest of the class combined. However, as camp was close to wrapping up, he would call us into his room at the end of the barracks and treat us to a shot or two of whiskey and some of his war stories.

One Saturday night we went to a rather drab hall on post, which was set aside just for the officer trainees. We drank gallons of reduce-alcohol beer and listened to the jukebox. The highlight of the evening was when the two New Yorkers got up and danced together to the Rolling Stones "(I Can't Get No) Satisfaction."

Midway through our training, I received a rude awakening when we were all treated to a live fire demonstration of "platoon in attack mode." The incredibly loud sound of the handheld bazookas and the jeep-mounted recoilless rifles scared the living bejesus out of me. Everywhere, the air became drenched with the pungent smell of cordite released from all the gunpowder. My only thought was to be thankful I was not in the infantry.

Uncle Marries Nephew

I had my bachelor party the night before the wedding. Mother took me out to a local bar. It was a lovely evening. She filled the conversation with anecdotes of my growing up. My parents rented a function room for the wedding at a local golf club and provided plenty of basic food, beer, wine, and a pretty good little band.

The wedding went off well. My uncle, "Father" Jack, had readily agreed to marry us, despite the complication of an imminent childbirth. Sandy showed very little of her seven months' pregnancy and looked great in her white gown.

Everyone danced at the wedding. Grampa Collins and Sandy's grandfather from Germany got along splendidly over many beers.

With my hitchhiking days behind me, I drove our little red Volkswagen to Acadia National Park in northern Maine for our honeymoon. Our dining out was mainly eating lobster at picnic tables.

Three Guys and Three Babies

I received orders to report in March to Fort Gordon, Georgia, for officer MP school. That was eight months away and I didn't have any employment in the meanwhile. The things they don't tell you! After the school, it would be off to Nuremburg, Germany.

This delay created a major cash-flow problem. I managed to get a few bucks coming in by driving a cab and reconciling bank statements for a local accountant. We rented an extremely inexpensive apartment in the slums of South Providence. The place was so bad that the landlord personally collected the rent each month. One time I went into the basement to check the fuse box. I wondered what a mattress was doing next to a coal bin. I found out later that a hooker was conducting her business there.

Our son Dylan was born on October 12, the night before we were to take a trip with friends to view the foliage in New Hampshire. In November, I landed a good-paying part-time job with United Parcel Service, loading and unloading trucks at night from two to six a.m. Sandy was able to get steady work as a substitute teacher shortly thereafter.

When I came home in the morning from UPS, it was time for Sandy to leave; so I changed and fed Dylan and then we were both able to have a couple of hours of sleep together. My mother-in-law was convinced I would roll over and smother him.

Don and another friend, Mickey Klitzner, were in similar situations. We met regularly, pushing our baby carriages around Roger Williams Park. We even started a weekly poker game during the day. High chairs, playpens, and baby bottles were brought to each game.

Later that fall we discovered that my friend Frank had moved into an apartment on the next street over with his bride, Debbie.

They invited us to a New Year's Eve party. We brought Dylan and his swing with us. In my mind, the swing was one of the best child-raising inventions of the century. The baby was placed in a hammock-like canvas seat, and like a wind-up toy, you just had to turn the crank several times to start its rocking motion.

Dylan was happy just sitting in the swing, but when the party got loud, he started crying. I cranked up the swing and he was asleep in a minute. Throughout the night, anytime someone went by the swing and saw that it was not rocking, they would crank it up. I understand they make baby swings with electric motors these days.

I was really fortunate to have had the time to spend with Dylan before going on active duty. Most men at that time never had the opportunity take such an active role in the early stage of fatherhood.

Chapter 18

Military Police School

We left the ghetto at the beginning of March. Sandy stopped her substitute teaching, and she and Dylan moved in with Sandy's mother and grandfather in North Providence.

Shortly thereafter I boarded a train in Providence bound for Fort Gordon in Augusta, Georgia, for nine weeks of training. I wore my khaki uniform, complete with the crossed-pistols insignia of an MP officer. During my layover in Washington, I was approached by an Army private who asked me to help him break up a fight in the men's room between two other enlisted men. I remembered that it was a big no-no for an enlisted man to strike an officer, so I confidently entered the men's room and started tongue-lashing the combatants. To my amazement, they stopped bloodying each other and snapped to attention. The train to Augusta was so jammed I ended up sitting on the bathroom floor, crowded next to another GI.

MP school wasn't too bad. I loved the Southern breakfasts of country ham and grits and picked up quite a taste for bourbon at the officers' club. The first thing we were taught was that an MP, particularly an officer, has to always look sharp, with a crisply starched and ironed uniform, spit-polished shoes that you could see your reflection in, and a polished brass belt buckle and insignia.

As an alumnus of the Goon Platoon at BC, this was a problem for me. The idea of working on my shoes every day annoyed me. I don't remember how, but I discovered a spray polish. While others worked hard on their shoes every night, it took me one minute to spray my shoes to a glossy finish.

We formed up for inspection first thing every morning. One morning, while I was in line and adjusting my belt buckle, I saw that my shoes had become totally white. I couldn't believe it! They were black when I left the barracks.

As I was receiving a loud reprimand from our instructor, my classmates were doing their damnedest not to break into laughter. It seems that after a week or so, you should apply polish or the spray hits raw leather and turns white. From then on, I had to perform the laborious task of spit-shining my shoes and boots.

The Cheater

In basic training at Fort Devens, I had done quite well on the rifle range. However, MPs also had to be proficient with a .45-caliber pistol. My ego took a beating on the pistol range. There were three of us who could not get the minimum-required score. I could barely even hit the target. We were given one more shot at it. We wouldn't get our weekend passes if we failed and would have to return to the range.

I fired off my shots and deliberately missed the target. When I got to the paper on the target, I pulled out a pencil and rapidly punched holes in the paper target. I was careful not to give myself too good of a score.

Midway through the school we were informed that a guest speaker from OPO in Washington would address us the next day. I had no idea what OPO was and did not bother to ask. That night, President Johnson went on television and informed the nation he was significantly adding troops to Operation Rolling Thunder in Vietnam from 200,000 to 400,000.

OPO is the Office of Personnel Operations. Major "OPO" appeared first thing in the morning and read off each name and their new assignment. Just about the whole class was rerouted to Vietnam. I was to report to Fort Benning, Georgia, and join the newly formed 552nd MP company, affectionately called the Nickel, Nickel, Deuce.

Oh, and by the way, Sandy was pregnant with our second child.

The Army allowed you to defer your deployment to Vietnam to be at the birth of a child. Sandy and I agonized over the situation. Ultimately, we felt it was better for my well-being to stay with the unit I would be training with; Sandy was

Lieutenant Dobbyn in uniform with Dylan

comfortable with the level of support on the home front from my large family and her mother. I was required to spend no more than twelve months in-country, and we wanted to get it behind us.

After a few days at home, I flew down to Columbus, Georgia, and checked into Fort Benning. After a couple of weeks, I returned home to bring Sandy and Dylan back down to stay with me for the duration of the training.

Road Trip

We packed up the Volkswagen and headed south. With the back seat folded down, the back of the car became a playpen for Dylan, then six months old, to crawl around and sleep in. Baby car seats and safety belts were not standard equipment at that time.

We got as far as the middle of Connecticut before the VW's engine lost most of its power. I have absolutely no mechanical ability or knowledge. The garage mechanic said something about a block and compression. He said he could fix it and have it ready for us in the morning. We stayed in a motel for the night and the car was ready to go in the morning. We headed south and the car was running fine until about the middle of New Jersey. The mechanic there said he could do a temporary fix, which could probably get us to Georgia. I had him do the work because we did not have enough cash to buy a new car.

The car ran well enough on a flat surface and was great going downhill. We barely made it to Richmond, Virginia, though. At that point we realized we would have to get a loan from the family or friends for a down payment on a used or new car. I found a Volkswagen dealership and we checked into the motel closest to it. I hoped a short driving test would not show the lack of compression and hurt the trade-in value.

I drove to the VW dealership the next morning and asked them what it would cost to get a new VW. They had someone check our car out for trade-in. I don't know what they did or didn't do, but they offered more than I hoped for. The salesman said that because I was an Army officer, I could get a loan from a local bank to finance the list price of the car. All I would need to provide was a $500 down payment.

I called Papa Dobbyn. "Hi, Papa. It's Ricky. How are you?"

"Whadda you need?" he answered.

"I need to borrow five hundred dollars," I replied.

"Where are you?" he asked.

"I'm in Richmond, Virginia."

"Give me the wiring information and I will get it right to you."

He didn't ask why I needed it or when I would pay him back. I paid him back after the Army gave me a few paychecks. Many years later, I learned from my aunt Ethel that he told everybody in the family how pleasantly surprised he was not only to be paid promptly, but that I paid him at all. Evidently, this was not common in our family.

By the afternoon we were on the highway headed south, driving a new Volkswagen. The bank processed the loan that morning, and the big shocker was that I was able to register the car in about thirty minutes, thanks to short lines and very nice people.

In the middle of the Carolinas, I was pulled over by a state trooper. I had been traveling well over the limit. He asked me where I was going in such a hurry. I told him I was reporting to duty at Fort Benning. I was amazed when he told me to just slow down a little and then went back to his car.

The ease with which I was able to purchase and register our new car and the lack of a ticket from the state trooper led me to recognize the respect our people have for those in the military.

Chapter 19

Heat, Drama, and Training

We arrived in Columbus a couple of days before I had to report into the 552nd Military Police Company. There were many temporary, furnished apartments available near Fort Benning. We found a nice one with a pool area and we were able to move right in.

Fort Benning was huge and made Fort Devens look like Fort Apache. I checked into the company and met my new boss and his staff. Captain Brennan, the company commander (CO), was from the Midwest. He had a baby face with sugar-bowl ears and a sort of "what, me worry?" demeanor. The Company First Sergeant McLean (Top) was right out of a John Wayne movie. He was brash with a confident air and made it clear right away that first sergeants outranked second lieutenants. He had already spent one tour in Vietnam.

The executive officer (XO) was a first lieutenant from Richmond. He was fresh out of law school and he looked like and sounded like the rooster cartoon character Foghorn Leghorn. "I say, I say!"

My job was leader of the 3rd Platoon. Sergeant Aguirre was

my platoon sergeant. He was calm and collected and was the oldest soldier in the company. He had been in the infantry in WWII and had fought in the Battle of the Bulge. He had also been in the Korean War. I had lucked out.

My three squad leaders were led by newly minted corporals—the squad members were mainly draftees just out of MP school and primarily from the inner city and rural areas.

Midsummer weather in South Georgia was like nothing I had ever experienced. The training regimen was not adjusted for the blistering heat. As it turned out, prickly heat rashes, chigger bites, and pygmy rattlesnakes were all good training for Vietnam's environment.

Initially, we had generalized physical training, including long marches. I tried chewing tobacco on one march, became dizzy, and nearly lost my lunch.

Military police work is no different from civilian police work. However, in a war zone, the major MP mission is security. Specifically, that meant preventing and subduing enemy terrorist and guerilla attacks on military facilities and transportation routes. Our training exercises concentrated on learning how guerrillas (Viet Cong) operated and included a replica of a Vietnam village. We also kicked up a lot of red clay dust, running convoy escort exercises through the Georgia woods.

Our CO seemed hesitant to give specific orders, and when he did give orders, they usually lacked specifics. That did not present a problem for me because, as Mother had said, I did not take orders well. Our platoon had some bright, natural leaders to whom I gave free rein. Oddly enough, I believe this garnered the admiration of my CO.

Drama

One evening Foghorn Leghorn called a clandestine meeting of the platoon leaders. The second platoon leader, Larry, a spit-and-polish type, kicked off the meeting. He complained that our commander was basically incompetent and might get us killed in the combat zone. Ted, who led the 1st platoon, was a quiet get-along kind of guy. True to form, he did not say much. It became apparent that this group had met previously when they both nodded at Foghorn's suggestion to go over the CO's head and report his ineptitudes to his boss.

In my opinion, they were overreacting. My position was that my men and I could work around any lack of, or stupid, decisions. I suggested we take our concerns directly to the CO. Top had already served one tour in Vietnam and seemed to know what he was doing. He could manage the CO.

Foghorn set up a meeting with our leader. We were in the field and gathered in his tent on folding chairs around a portable wooden table. The CO, without hesitation, asked what the problem was. We all looked at each other, waiting for someone to speak. With frustration in his voice, he asked again.

Since nobody said anything, I impulsively spoke up for the group. "The problem is with you," I said, with full expectation that the others would join in with specifics. I don't remember what was said by the others after that, but it wasn't much.

Instantly, I went from being in his good graces to somebody he loathed. I'd like to say I learned a life lesson, but my big impulsive mouth still remains a problem.

An Hour at the Beach

I got time on the weekends to spend with Sandy and Dylan. We hung out at the pool and attempted to cool off by dipping ourselves and Dylan in water that was hot enough to cook a lobster. It felt wonderful to go back inside to the air-conditioning in the apartment.

We took advantage of a long weekend and drove south to Panama City on the Gulf of Mexico. We arrived in the evening and checked into a small shack right on the beach. We went to the beach first thing in the morning, hoping to beat the heat and enjoy a breeze off the Gulf.

There was no breeze, and at nine in the morning, we were burning up just sitting on the blanket. We packed up and drove right back to the air-conditioned apartment.

Our unit's September departure was closing in. At the end of August, I was granted several days' leave and Sandy, Dylan, and I headed north. My mother had secured a small apartment for Sandy in Warren, Rhode Island, a town next to my family in Bristol. It was adequately furnished but needed a new bed.

With only a few more days together, we immediately headed to a furniture store. It was a large store, and as we entered, a salesman headed our way. He spoke directly to Sandy and asked how he could help us. She told him we needed a bed quickly because I was leaving for Vietnam.

At the top of his lungs, he yelled out to the bed department: "Hey, Bobby! This lady needs a bed right away; her husband is going to Vietnam." Everybody in the store looked our way, and I think we may have been blushing.

After I left for 'Nam, my sister Chrissy moved in with Sandy and stayed until I returned. She was a great help to her when Eric was born, and later babysat. This allowed Sandy the opportunity to land a weekend cocktail-pianist gig at a nearby restaurant.

Hurry up and Wait

After three months' training, the 552nd was ready to ship out. However, the departure date was delayed for at least a week. This made everyone anxious and wondering what to do in the meantime.

During the delay, we worked the troops hard with long marches and physical exercises. My favorite was fighting with pugil sticks. Pugil sticks are wooden poles with padding on each end. They replicate fighting with a bayonet. After watching the men pummel one another for a while, I challenged Ted to a duel. The two platoons gathered around us, cheering and trash-talking while we battled. I was bigger than Ted and expected to win pretty quickly. It turned out that he was very strong and wily. We fought until we could hardly breathe or raise our arms. It was a draw. The troops loved it.

Our evenings were free, and Phoenix City, just across the river in Alabama, was a notorious GI hangout. Top was familiar with the town and led us on several expeditions. The dangerous thing was that the clubs did not serve liquor, but one could bring one's own bottle and buy the mixers. I invariably overserved myself. After a long evening with Mr. Jack Daniel's at a nightclub and two hours of sleep, I awoke for reveille as the sun rose. They told me my morning address to the platoon was a bit of a rant about them slacking off and not being tough enough. I woke up later that afternoon thankful to those who had escorted me back to bed. I was very pleased when instructions for our departure finally arrived. I am sure not everyone was excited to go to war. But I really just wanted to get this whole ordeal over with.

Chapter 20

The Cruise

After our bumpy, uncomfortable plane ride from Georgia, we landed at Oakland International Airport and were shuttled over to the Port of Oakland, where we boarded the transport vessel USNS *Buckner*. This was her third war; she had served in WWII and Korea.

Living conditions aboard the ship for an officer were luxurious compared to those for enlisted men. Officers had their own cabins, furnished with bunk beds. The enlisted men slept in hammocks crammed together in the hold of the vessel. Officers also had their own spacious dining room, replete with white tablecloths.

My roommate was Mr. Spit and Polish, the second platoon leader. His demeaner put me off. Larry had gone from being scared to death that the CO would get us all killed to sucking up to him big-time. When I arrived at the cabin, he had already laid claim to the bottom bunk. He could not wait to show me his newly purchased .357 Magnum pistol and a bowie knife, as if special weaponry would ensure his safety.

The ship was still tied to the dock when he started getting

seasick. He remained seasick for a week or so. It didn't help that a guest or two would join me for cocktails before dinner in our cabin. All he could do was lie in his bunk eating crackers while we imbibed.

The next day we arrived in San Diego and the Marines came aboard. That night only officers were allowed to go ashore. I took advantage and hit the closest sailors' dive for few drinks.

Initially, life on board was uneventful and quite pleasurable. My only duty was to accompany an old grizzled Navy lieutenant commander on his early-morning inspections of the troop's quarters. His breath reeked of booze. I drew comfort from the fact that I wasn't the only one in violation of the Navy's regulation of no alcohol on board.

The greater part of the afternoon was spent reading and playing poker. I held my own for a while, but eventually ran out of cash and had to sell some of my liquor stock to keep playing.

I loved to go to the very bow of the ship when were in high seas and rough weather. It was like being in an elevator. Falling asleep in my bunk to the up-and-down rhythm of the sea was a comforting feeling.

The ship docked for refueling at White Beach Naval Facility in Okinawa. It was not a deep-water port, but rather a beautiful beach with a very long pier. Officers were allowed to go ashore for the day and enlisted men for the afternoon. The officers' club was perched on a cliff above the beach and the enlisted men's club was right on the beach.

I had a nice lunch at the officers' club and developed a pleasant buzz at the bar, when I was verbally accosted from behind by the CO.

"Lieutenant! Things are getting out of control on the beach. Report immediately back to the ship. Marine Lieutenant Casper will meet you there. The two of you must get all the men back aboard ship immediately!"

I carefully navigated the deep stairs to the beach and was able to get a good view of the "things getting out of control." Men were rolling around in the surf, half passed out, and fights were breaking out all over the place between the Army and the Marines. I raced down the beach, boarded the ship, and went to my cabin. I put my MP armband on upside down and headed out to find Lieutenant Casper.

Casper was waiting for me at the gangplank. We both looked at each other with the same *how the hell did we get this job?* expression and exchanged pleasantries on our way down the dock. We methodically worked our way down the beach, instructing men to help us get everyone out of the water and back onto the ship. We busted up a couple of fights along the way. When we entered the enlisted men's club, the entire floor was soaked in beer, and much of the furniture was in splinters. Interservice fisticuffs were still in progress. We decided that it was past the time for intervention and it was best to let things work themselves out. We pushed our way to the corner of the bar, grabbed a couple of beers, and toasted our brilliant strategy.

Several veteran sergeants, Marine and Army, were key in herding the men back onto the ship. No one was seriously injured that day, even the guys who jumped into the water off the fantail of the ship. I later learned that troops on military vessels heading to Vietnam and docking at White Beach were never again allowed to go ashore.

Civil War

After the brawling on the beach, the attitude of the men back on board ship had changed. I could feel the interservice hostility bubbling under the surface that, along with racism, would soon lead to the attack and wounding of a Marine enlisted man.

Two white Marine Southerners were tormenting a black Army private who was on KP duty in the ship's mess. The private defended himself with a kitchen knife, severely wounding one of the Marines.

Twenty-four-hour MP patrols were established immediately. An investigation was underway, and the ship's brig was activated for two prisoners. Our card games, lounging on the fantail, and cocktail hour came to an abrupt end.

This horrible and totally unnecessary incident served to remind everyone who the real enemy was and that we would be meeting them very soon.

Our first stop was Da Nang, a large port city in the middle of the Vietnam coast. The ship docked early in the morning, and the Marine battalion disembarked. The trip usually took seventeen to eighteen days, but we had been at sea for twenty-one days because one of the ship's propellers was out of commission.

Here We Go!

After we left Da Nang, word came down that we would arrive the next day at a place called Vung Tau. That was pretty much all the information we received. I asked around and nobody else had a clue as to what would be involved. Theories ran from a D-Day scenario to a cruise-ship-like docking in Nassau. I briefed my platoon and basically told them that details would be forth-coming and to be dressed in full combat gear with guns loaded.

It turned out to be a combination of both D-Day and Nassau. It resembled D-Day in that we climbed down rope netting on the side of the ship into LSTs (landing craft) that took us to shore, but it was like Nassau in that nobody was shooting at us and when the gate of the LST opened up we were on a lovely beach! We were met by an Army greeting committee, photographers, and kids selling Cokes.

We were hustled onto a C-130 aircraft and flown to Bien Hoa, twenty miles northeast of Saigon (now Ho Chi Minh City). Our ship continued on up the river to the Port of Saigon, where our jeeps and equipment were to be unloaded.

When we disembarked from the plane, I felt a sense of relief. Not having a clue as to what to expect, one tends to fear the worst. The journey was over, and I was standing safely on Viet-namese soil, at least for now.

Chapter 21

Long Binh

Our final destination was a base camp in Long Binh, a few miles outside of Bien Hoa. The base was a pile of dirt surrounded by barbed wire. We were all pleasantly surprised that large tents with canvas cots inside had already been set up for our immediate use. There were around twelve men per tent.

The next day a group of us were trucked to the Saigon docks. We each returned driving a jeep stacked with wooden pallets. The pallets were to serve as a floor to the tents. They kept us dry and created an adequate, but not foolproof, separation from the rat population. We learned to sleep with our hands on the cot, not dangling down, to avoid being bitten. It certainly beat sleeping in the jungle. (Over the course of the war, Long Binh became a huge base headquarters with permanent buildings, including a hospital and a prison.)

Perimeter protection guard duty was our first job. This did not go well. In the middle of the night, one of our guards was spooked and opened fire on the engineering water purification point just outside the camp's barbed wire. The engineers guarding the water point fired back, and a firefight ensued for a few minutes. Nobody was hurt, but as I will explain later, engineering support was not easily available to us trigger-happy MP newbies.

Headquarters security and convoy escort were our main jobs. New units were coming in all the time and needed to be brought to base camps and kept supplied.

The CO's animosity toward me seemed to increase over time. His new pet was "Seasick Larry" and his highly polished belt buckle. He was assigned to the headquarters security detail. *Better to look good than to be good!* I was assigned to head up convoy escort and also received the not-so-highly coveted appointment as the company sanitation officer.

Dobbyn's Folly

I quietly laughed off the sanitation assignment…until I got an order to actually do something. After each rain, the dirt eroded everywhere, and the tubes used as urinals were starting to back up. A water-drainage system of some sort was sorely needed.

Since we were not fully deployed yet, some men had time available. Everyone had been issued entrenching tools (shovels). I foolishly believed I was smart enough to create a drainage area because I had helped to build a leeching field and install a septic tank for our summer home at Horseneck Beach.

I drew lines in the dirt with a stick and judged the grade by eye. Throughout the scorching heat of the day, my men used their entrenching tools to very diligently dig narrow ditches away from the tents, the shit houses, and the pee tubes. At day's end it all looked good to me.

However, after the first rain, the ditches disappeared and created pond-like sewage pools—everywhere. The drainage was worse than before. The CO was ecstatic over my total failure. But I was not to be deterred and confidently told him I would get the job done correctly.

I decided to get a couple bottles of bourbon and visit the engineers at the water point. After they busted my balls regarding the recent firefight with our MPs, they took the bourbon and agreed to visit the next day with a man and a machine. They even designed the drainage layout and helped us to complete the project with a minimum of labor. Dobbyn's Folly had been transformed into a functioning drainage system.

On-the-Job Training

I was sent over to the 173rd Airborne Brigade to observe how their MPs ran convoy escort missions. Everyone who has ever been in the Army knows the superiority complex airborne troops have over the regular troops, known as Legs. I don't blame them. Who is willing to jump out of a perfectly fine aircraft carrying a rifle, ammo, and a heavy rucksack while being shot at?

I arrived at chow time and met my counterpart, Lieutenant Sousa. He was pleasant and wasted very little time getting down to business. He explained what they had been doing and how they handled the problems they encountered. Rule number one was: when getting fired upon, keep moving as fast as you can. That was also rule number two, three, et cetera. He also explained that when encountering a roadblock, throw a boat anchor and line over the blockade and drag it through to set off any explosives that had been planted. Later, I passed that information to our motor-pool sergeant. He went into Bien Hoa and bought an anchor and line for every jeep.

I didn't sleep well that night thinking that the next day might be my first experience at being shot at. Before daybreak, I met up with the convoy and was assigned to ride with Sousa's Sergeant First Class Middleton. He kept an unlit cigar in his mouth and wore a ball cap instead of a helmet. He exuded confidence and lowered my apprehension. His driver was a sarcastic tank-shaped fellow. I enjoyed listening to their banter about them having the onerous assignment of having to babysit a Leg officer for the day.

I sat in the back of the jeep, and after we had started moving along, I noticed that their flak vests were hung on the back of their seats. It had been beaten into my head to *always wear the flak vest*. They explained how the damned things were too hot and they never wore them, but they did make a good back cushion. After a while we slowed down for a sharp curve in the road. Middleton explained that while they were on patrol, a couple of Viet Cong had attacked them from the brush. In the fray of the battle, Lieutenant Sousa had blown away a Viet Cong from up close with his pistol. I didn't ask how close "up close" was and hoped to hell I would never experience any such closeness.

The Road Runner

When I returned to my company, I learned that in seven days I was to lead a convoy of large supply vehicles called bridge trucks. The destination was Xuan Loc, about thirty miles north of Long Binh in the foothills. The immediate problem for this mission was that we did not have any mounts for the machine guns. What were the logistic clowns in the Pentagon thinking? Fortunately, our motor-pool crew was creative and bought metal piping in nearby Bien Hoa. The pipes were welded to the middle of the jeep, and the machine gun was attached. The gun was set at a height so that a gunner could stand up to fire.

It took a while to prove out the original prototype. Much to the amusement of everyone, the machine guns kept falling over backward when the jeeps started moving. The heavier .50-caliber machine gun took the most work.

My men with machine-gun jeeps ready to start first convoy escort

I started wondering what we should do if we were attacked and needed help. At this point, I had not received any instructions from anyone. It turned out nobody else had given it a thought. Every jeep had a radio, but we only knew the frequency of our company. I brought this up to the CO and Top. They eventually got back to me with the frequency for the helicopter, medevac, to evacuate the wounded, and said they would coordinate any additional firepower needed. I felt much better knowing all that, but I realized if I had to ask these questions, our leadership was lacking.

The convoy had three machine-gun jeeps. One M60 .30-caliber was on point, running as a scout ahead of the convoy. Another M60 was in the middle. The heavy .50-caliber gun was in the last jeep. The rear wheels on the jeep were bent out by the weight of the gun. None of our guns had been test fired from the jeeps. I was really worried that the mount for the .50-caliber gun would collapse and end up on the road.

My driver and I were a couple of trucks back in the convoy. I was pleased to have been armed with a grenade launcher, a shotgun-type weapon that shoots grenades shaped like large bullets. This was the perfect weapon for someone like me, who could not hit the side of a barn with a pistol from twenty feet away.

The only disturbing thing that morning was when we came upon an armored personnel carrier (APC) by the side of the road. It was burned out and still smoldering. I got on the radio and gave the order to get the convoy moving as fast as possible. When we got to the base camp in Xuan Loc, I found out that the Second of the 34th Armor had been keeping the road open with armored personnel carriers.

I spoke with a soldier who said he was glad he ran the road in an armored vehicle instead of in an unprotected jeep. I thought of the smoldering APC and could not imagine being trapped inside. I told him we just arrived on the backs of their work. Once again, the lack of communication was scary. It amazed me that no one had mentioned that an armored unit was also working the road.

Sometimes we stayed over in order to escort a convoy back to Long Binh. One night in the Xuan Loc base camp we came under an intermittent mortar attack. The base camp was in the shadow of a small mountain. I learned that mortar attacks from the mountain were not an uncommon event.

The man huddled next to me along the row of sandbags said "Puff the Magic Dragon" would put an end to this attack shortly. Puff turned out to be a C130 aircraft. This turboprop cargo plane was modified to carry .50-caliber Gatling guns along one side so that it could slowly circle over a target area and shoot the hell out of it. It was an awesome sight. I couldn't imagine how any living thing could survive such an attack. The recurrence of these mortar attacks from the mountain puzzled me until I learned about the tunnels and underground shelters that the enemy had constructed.

Puff the Magic Dragon

Good News and a Haircut

In mid-October, the company clerk informed me that he received notification from the Red Cross that on October fourth, my wife gave birth to a baby boy and that both were doing well. In those days, the only communication available from home was by mail, and I had been waiting nervously for a letter from Sandy. I was not aware that the Red Cross had the job of handling personal messages.

Although I was tremendously relieved to finally get the good news about Sandy and Dylan's new brother, Eric, I couldn't help but wonder why it took the Red Cross so long to inform me.

I later encountered the Red Cross's program of sending an attractive young lady to visit. She played cards with the off-duty soldiers that day and then was helicoptered away. Maybe it's just me, but I felt visits like that (*The Bob Hope Show* included) just pushed everyone's testosterone to uncomfortable levels.

The base camp was growing rapidly. New troops were arriving all the time and the base population was getting into the thousands. Wooden buildings were cropping up all over. We got a shower hutch, our own outhouse, and our own mess hall. Oil barrels were used in all the outhouses. The waste disposal system consisted of pouring fuel oil into the barrels and burning the contents. Every morning black shit-filled smoke permeated the air throughout the base and the countryside.

Local civilian personnel were employed to work inside the base camp. They helped with cleaning buildings and equipment, filled sandbags, and provided services like laundry, boot shining, and haircuts. I had my hair cut by a local barber and was initially a little nervous when he used his straight-edged razor. He also massaged my neck and shoulders and finished by cracking my neck like a chiropractor. It felt good.

Mrs. Tran was our laundry service provider. She traveled a twenty-mile trip from Saigon two or three times a week in her three-wheeled van/motorcycle to pick up and deliver the laundry. She spoke excellent English and I learned that she and her husband were Catholics and had fled the North when the Communists took over. They had four sons. More about them later…

A Python and a Chess Game

While serving as night-duty officer, I received a call from the guard at the front-gate bunker. He reported that a large snake was crawling past his post into the base. My driver, PFC Grubbs, was a country boy from Texas. Together, we drove over to the Transportation Company located near the gate. A ten-foot-long python was drawing a crowd of fascinated but apprehensive soldiers. A second lieutenant was moving in on the snake with his .45-caliber pistol at the ready.

Grubbs and I got out of the jeep and headed toward the snake. For "safety" reasons, I followed behind him. The snake was still slowly sliding along when the lieutenant took a shot at its head and missed. He was only a few feet away and his hand was shaking badly. He kept firing and missing until he emptied the gun.

Grubbs then fired one shot from his rifle and the snake was dead. I commiserated with the lieutenant because I couldn't have done much better with that pistol. Grubbs insisted on taking the snake back to our unit. He wanted to skin it and have boots made. He suggested we give the meat to the Vietnamese, who would love it. I told him that sounded great, but in no way was I touching that thing. He and a couple of men draped the carcass over the hood of the jeep. When we got back to our unit, he laid the snake over a row of sandbags and went to work skinning the snake and slicing up the meat. The next morning, he brought the snake meat to Bien Hoa for distribution.

Early one evening the company clerk burst into the beer tent and told me that I had a phone call. My heart hit my throat, fearing bad news from home.

I ran to the headquarters tent and picked up the headset. "Hello. Who is this?"

"It's me…Pap." Paul Arnold Pellini, "Pap," my good friend and college roommate. I knew he had been drafted and was an enlisted man in the Army. I had no idea he was in Vietnam. He was a clerk and handled his unit's communication, so he was able to get patched through to my unit.

As we started talking, I began feeling the urge to pee. As the conversation continued, I realized I might have a decision to make: cut the call short or piss my pants. We shared experiences and agreed to start a chess game via the mail. At least only the company clerk was able to witness the pee running down my leg and all over the floor.

We mailed moves back and forth to each other for the length of our stay. At one point in the game, he contested one of my moves because one of his pieces occupied the space I was trying to take. I thought it over and agreed with him. In hindsight, we agreed that both of us must have been a bit buzzed because my move to take his piece was legitimate.

Eventually, we met back in the States and finished the match at my house. It kills me to say it: Pap won.

Metal Rain

One evening just after dark, I heard a big boom, quickly followed by others. In the distance, a huge mushroom-shaped cloud rose up. Okay, this is it! The decades-long fear of a nuclear attack had materialized. Why look for shelter? The shock wave would get us in a few seconds and the radiation would fry us after that.

Pieces of metal were dropping from the sky in all directions. I ran into a tent and tried to become one with a sandbag. I came out of the tent when the booms and the shrapnel shower ended. I didn't know what was happening. I rushed my platoon to the edge of the perimeter facing the direction of the explosion to stop a potential penetration of our base camp. One soldier ahead of me seemed to be hesitating and was moving slowly. I kicked him in the butt and yelled at him. The kick was not necessary and was against regulations. I think my adrenaline got the best of me.

But there was no attack on our base. Unbeknownst to most of us, there was an ammunition dump a mile or so down a side road behind the base camp. I emphasize was, because Viet Cong infiltrated the perimeter and planted satchels of explosives throughout the base, blowing it all to pieces.

Ammo dump explosion

May I Have the Grenade?

I was night-duty officer again when a call for assistance came in from the Transportation Company. When Grubbs and I arrived, we jumped out of the jeep and joined the crowd that had gathered next to and behind several trucks. About thirty yards away, a really young-looking private was standing in front of a tent holding a hand grenade. A sergeant came up to me and explained that the private was threatening to pull the pin and blow himself up. In MP school, we received situational training for various domestic and related disturbances. But none of them involved a suicidal kid with a hand grenade.

The transportation sergeant on duty filled me in on the private's personal information. He was Emmet Bailey from Carolina Beach, North Carolina, and had been warned many times about his lack of sobriety.

I walked slowly toward him and said: "Emmet, I'm Lieutenant Dobbyn. How are you doing? They tell me you're from Carolina Beach."

He replied, "Ah just don't give a goddam, sir." I could tell he was totally inebriated.

Usually it is not hard to deal with that condition; however, he was holding the grenade in his right hand and his left hand was on the pin. I kept talking and walking until I was right in front of him. I had to concentrate to keep my voice from cracking with fear. After more conversation, which seemed to go on forever, he gave me the grenade. The sergeant gently led the crying private away. My hands shook violently for quite a while after I safely handed off the grenade.

Bullets and BBQ

I received orders to make a convoy run to Ben Cat, which was about thirty-five miles northwest of Long Binh. A classmate from MP school was stationed there. Rod was from Texas. With his strong jaw, blond hair, and blue eyes, he looked like the hero of a Hollywood Western. Several of my other classmates were in-country or would be shortly.

Rod greeted me like a long-lost brother. He was excited to tell me that Hank Williams Jr. had arrived in camp and was going to put on a show that night. I was underwhelmed. Country music was not my favorite.

We had shots of bourbon for cocktail hour. Rod cooked on a barbecue grill made from a barrel and we feasted on a Texas-sized steak washed down with several cans of Australian panther piss called Swan Lager. We kept drinking during the show, and even as numb as I was, I was not enjoying the music. I kept my feelings to myself and feigned enthusiasm for Rod's sake.

I woke the next morning with an awful headache. The convoy formed up just after daybreak. We encountered small-arms fire on the way back. I was enraged that the Viet Cong would dare attack me in my exhausted and strung-out condition. We sped up as fast as possible and the machine-gun jeeps returned fire. Nobody got hurt.

When we drove up to the motor pool, one of the mechanics pointed out a large bullet hole that entered one side of the jeep and went out the other. It had passed within inches of our posteriors.

Happy Holidays

I spent Christmas Eve of 1966 sitting on the hood of a jeep that was stuck in a rice patty. Second Platoon Private Scungio had "borrowed" a jeep and had driven in the direction of a nearby village. He must have passed out driving, because he was found unconscious at the wheel of the jeep in the rice paddy. I volunteered to stay and guard the jeep. My driver took Scungio back to the base and returned later with a tow truck.

There was no sign of a reindeer that Christmas Eve, but I had a water buffalo to keep me company. Make that bad company, because they are very ornery critters. It was pitch-black and the beast was thrashing around near me. I kept my .45-caliber pistol in its holster and relied upon a World War II–era "grease gun" that I had bought on the black market. It shot .45-caliber rounds on automatic, but with little accuracy.

Scungio was gone from our unit the next day. His punishment was to be assigned to an infantry unit as an infantryman, not an MP. Infantry units were taking very heavy casualties at that time.

A few weeks later, a letter from my mother arrived, informing me that Papa had died. I didn't know until I returned home that Papa Dobbyn had died on that Christmas Eve. His influence on me as a boy and young man stayed with me throughout my life.

Stupid Games

The CO periodically held a staff meeting that included the XO (Foghorn Leghorn), the three platoon leaders, and Top. The CO usually had little of consequence to say and, instead, let Top tell us what was happening and what we should do. However, at one meeting he took charge and stated that he was very concerned that we (the officers) were getting too friendly with the enlisted men. He said this was primarily due to the fact that we all drank beer together in the same tent. He instructed that an officers-only beer tent be built, so that we would not have to mingle and drink with the enlisted men.

The tent was set up, and for a few nights the two or so of us not on duty had a couple of beers with the CO and Foghorn Leghorn, boring the hell out of us. Sometimes Top would drop by for a beer or two, but overall attendance in the new "officers' club" was low. I started drifting over to the "enlisted club" under the pretense of having a couple of beers with Top and Sergeant Aguirre. The trouble was I would end up closing down the club, usually in the company of Top.

One night, Top challenged me to a game of "stretch." As a kid, I had played stretch with a jackknife, so why not a bayonet? You faced each other a few feet apart and took turns throwing a bayonet next to the other person's foot. If the bayonet stuck, you had to widen your stance to meet the bayonet. You won when your opponent could not stretch to the bayonet. Top won.

He showed me another "game." He placed his hand on the bar and then rapidly stuck the bayonet between each of his fingers. I was not to be outdone and gave it a try. I did it without cutting any fingers, but it was clear Top was much faster

Top had one more competitive event up his sleeve. He straightened his arm with his palm up and then placed a dollar bill on his wrist. With a lit cigarette, he burned five holes in the dollar bill without even flinching. *If he could handle it, so could I.*

It hurt like hell, but I did make five holes in the dollar…as well as five burn holes in my wrist. The men laughed their asses off when Top showed that his wrist was not burned. The trick was to make a fist, which created a hollow row between the ligaments in his wrist. Lesson learned: *Do not fuck around with a first sergeant.*

Chapter 22

Court-Martial?

I had run only a few convoys but began to wonder when some-body else would have the pleasure. I asked Top how one could request a transfer to another unit. He told me the Army had a form for everything, and all I had to do was fill it out and submit it to the CO. He would have to either approve or disapprove. Either way, the request had to be sent to the base commander. I filled out the form and gave it to him.

A week later, Top notified me that the CO had disapproved my request and the base commander had also disapproved it. I submitted the form every week for three weeks and every week the result was the same.

As punishment for my persistence in requesting transfer, the CO ordered me confined to the base unless I was on an assigned mission. That meant that the occasional visits to Bien Hoa to shop and enjoy the restaurants and bars were out.

One morning, the CO informed me that in one hour he would conduct an inspection of my platoon. I told him they had been on duty all night and were sleeping. He insisted anyway. I ordered Aguirre to wake everyone and get them ready for inspection.

My men were extremely annoyed, but Aguirre was nonplussed. After his many years in the Army, he was used to this silliness.

The CO started the inspection right on time. To their credit, everybody had cleaned up their tents, organized their gear, and were standing at attention next to their cots. The CO picked up an entrenching tool and pointed out that the olive-drab paint had worn off. He picked up another, which was in the same condition, and commented that bare metal could be spotted by the enemy. The fact was that we had no use for them except to dig rain gutters and holes for pee tubes. Even the infantry troops were never seen with them.

"Lieutenant, I want all the entrenching tools painted immediately, and I expect a report from you when they are done. That will be all." I watched him storm off, shaking my head in disbelief at the vindictiveness behind his order.

"There is no way I am going to order these men to work on this ridiculous project," I told Sergeant Aguirre.

He quickly replied, "Sir, disobeying a direct order in a combat zone is a really big deal. It's situations like this that remind me of how glad I am to be an enlisted man."

"Okay, Sarge; dismiss the men so they can get back to sleep," I answered as I walked out of the tent.

I went back to my tent to contemplate the situation. Captain Queeg, in the film *The Caine Mutiny*, came to mind. Queeg had turned his ship upside down in search of the culprit who had allegedly stolen a can of his strawberries.

In my mind the CO was worse than Queeg, in that his personal vendetta had a direct adverse effect on my entire platoon. Also, getting a can of strawberries back was more sensible than painting a shovel for no fucking reason.

My fear of retribution turned into *I don't give a goddam*. I marched down to the CO's tent and told him that if he wanted to get the shovels painted, he would have to give the order himself, because I was not going to.

He was shocked and immediately informed me he was reporting my actions to headquarters. Top whispered to me as I was leaving that I was in really deep doo-doo.

The next week, Top told me to accompany him to a meeting with our own Captain Queeg. Reckoning time had arrived. At least I wasn't in an orange jumpsuit or in cuffs to receive my sentencing.

Queeg stood rigid as he read the letter from headquarters. It went something like this. "Regarding the reported failure of Lieutenant Dobbyn to comply with a direct order from Captain Brennan, the Field Force One Commander General Hicken-looper has ordered that a letter of reprimand be placed in his personnel file."

I was almost giddy that I had received a punishment akin to ten lashes with a wet noodle. I went back to my tent and filled out another request-for-transfer form.

In MP school at Fort Gordon, I became friends with a fellow MP from Louisiana who was a grad from Loyola, in New Orleans. He mentioned that the MP general on General Westmoreland's staff was also a Loyola graduate. He had heard through family connections that the general was well liked on a personal level and was a good leader.

Somehow, I had it in my head that if you really wanted results, go to the top. Maybe it was from my mother, who had no qualms about summoning a store manager if she had a problem.

I verified that the commander of all MPs in Vietnam was the same general from New Orleans. He was stationed in the "Head Shed" in Saigon, which was presided over by General Westmoreland, the big kahuna.

In defiance of the order not to leave the base, I commandeered a jeep from the motor pool and headed off to the big city.

Finding headquarters was a major effort. Every American I asked kept getting me closer and closer. The heavy traffic of scooters, three-wheeled mini-trucks, bicycles, 1950s-era Renault taxis, pedicabs (trishaws), and military vehicles was daunting.

There was a very distinct, unforgettable odor to the streets of Saigon, probably a mixture of gasoline fumes and poor sanitation. Many men and women urinated in the street in plain sight.

I entered the headquarters building, which looked like it had previously been a mansion of some sort. A sergeant E9 (highest enlisted rank) guarded the entrance to the general's inner office. His demeanor and voice made me almost want to salute him. He had that "What the hell do you want?" look. I explained that I had come in from Long Binh and wanted to talk to the general about a personnel matter.

He went into the general's office, then came right back out and motioned to me to go in. I walked in slowly, filled with apprehension. I had never even seen a general before.

I saluted smartly and then blurted out, "Sir, you can throw me right out of here, but…"

"Damn right I can, Lieutenant! Now, what's on your mind?"

I explained that I had been trying to get a transfer to another unit and I didn't care which, even including an MP infantry unit. I told him that my commanding officer had it in for me, and the situation was at the point where my entire platoon was affected. I went on to mention his chickenshit actions and added that somehow, I was always the officer assigned to the riskier assignments.

I think I may not have been the first one to complain about Queeg. Without asking any questions, he made a slight smile and told me to file another request for transfer when I returned to my unit.

A week later Top rushed up to me with a paper in his hand. "I don't know how the fuck you did it, Dobbyn," he said with a smile as he handed me my orders. Effective immediately, I was assigned to C Company of the 716th MP battalion in Saigon.

Top arranged for a jeep and a driver to take me to Saigon. He also handed me my personnel file to turn in at my new unit head-quarters. Before I left, I thanked my men, especially Aguirre, for their good work. On the trip into Saigon, I removed the repri-mand letter from my personnel file and shredded it to pieces.

Chapter 23

Saigon

Many of the hotels in Saigon had been converted into US barracks. I was assigned to the Victoria Hotel, a billet for officers. The year before, the Viet Cong attacked the Victoria with guns, grenades, and a car bomb. The face of the hotel had been ripped off and the first four floors were reduced to rubble. Four MPs and four Vietnamese were killed, and seventy-two officers were injured. One of the MPs killed had been the CO of C Company. The hotel had been completely rebuilt by the time I arrived.

MP carrying wounded Vietnamese after Victoria Hotel attack

My room had a real bed with sheets and an overhead fan. I could not believe my good fortune. I placed a bottle of bourbon and a chaser of water on my bedside table and settled into bed with a book. I had barely made a dent in the bottle when my stomach started growling. I lunged for the toilet as volcanic eruptions shot out of both ends of my body. It was over as soon as it started. I discovered the French warning sign in the bathroom as I was cleaning up my mess. "*Ne pas boire l'eau.*" I then remembered that all the water I drank at Long Binh had been processed by the engineers' water depot.

A week later Lieutenant Conway, a burly college football player from North Carolina, became my roommate. He'd played halfback for Wake Forest but had the build of a lineman. His job was in transportation, including running the motor pool.

He had a good sense of humor. Every time I asked him how he was doing, he would blurt out in a thick Southern drawl, "Aw caint go own!" like some exhausted Southern belle.

"But you have to go on!" I always retorted. After a while he got me saying it.

Learning the Ropes

I received very thorough on-the-job training from a first lieutenant who had spent many months prowling the streets of Saigon. I discovered there were many dos and don'ts unique to duty-officer work in the "big city." The primary mission was anti-guerrilla warfare, specifically, to prevent terrorist attacks or to deal with the aftermath when they occurred. The police work with our own troops mainly involved protecting them, not policing them. I listened carefully and learned a lot. This new job was much more involved than convoy escort and, at times, more nerve-racking.

There was a military police station that was the communication center for all the MP patrols. All jeep patrols were assigned a district of the city. There were several patrols in each district with two men in each jeep. At least one of the patrols in each district had a jeep mounted with a machine gun.

We had an interpreter at the MP station who was Chinese and knew a couple of dialects, as well as Vietnamese and American English. He was amusing and very knowledgeable. One time he illustrated to me how the Mandarin symbol for a tree evolved over a thousand or so years. The first tree looked like a tree. The current tree was just three slashes.

A lieutenant, usually a platoon leader, was assigned as duty officer for each shift. The duty officer had operational control of all the men on duty at the station and in the streets. Most of the time on duty was spent driving around the city checking on guard posts, monitoring and issuing orders on the radio, and responding to the scene of incidents.

First Patrol

My first assignment was duty officer on the day shift. My driver was Arlo, a private from the hills of Tennessee. While we were on patrol in the center of the city, the dispatcher notified us that a GI had been attacked and badly injured in front of a restaurant near our location. When we arrived, the GI had already been taken away. I wondered if he would survive when I saw remnants of what he had for lunch on the sidewalk.

I joined the MP patrol inside the restaurant. They were

questioning the diners to determine who attacked the soldier. Witnesses reported that two young Vietnamese males rode by on a motor scooter and flipped a grenade at the soldier as he emerged from the restaurant.

I pulled out my notepad to prepare a report, but I couldn't write because my hand was shaking so badly. One of the MPs tactfully volunteered to take over. I was grateful and very embarrassed. Random attacks on individuals were common throughout the city.

The Viet Cong used indiscriminate bombing to terrorize the civilian population. They would choose locations where a large number of people gathered. The explosives were hidden in trash cans, carts, cars, and even stuffed in the metal tubes of bicycles.

A favorite sick trick was to plant two explosives. They timed the second one to go off after the first responders had arrived. Unfortunately, not all the first responders, both American and Vietnamese, were aware of this dirty trick. It was difficult to get the word out and, at the same time, have as many men as possible searching like crazy for the second explosive.

When an explosion, or an explosive device, was discovered, the Explosive Ordinance Disposal Unit (EOD), was called in. The closest MP patrol to the EOD personnel would rendezvous with the two-man team and get them to the scene as fast as possible. And did we go! Driving at high speed through the crowded city streets required horn honking, whistle blowing, and yelling *"di di mau"* (get out of the way!) at the top of our lungs.

Arlo and I did not work well together. Half the time I couldn't understand what he was saying. He probably did not understand my Boston accent the other half of the time. Also, on the late-night shifts, he tended to fall asleep at the wheel. He was replaced by Specialist Four Rollins, from New York City.

Celebrity Luncheon

Many civilians, visiting dignitaries, and celebrities stayed in the Meyercord Hotel. They had a small cafeteria for guests only. It was also the only place in Saigon where we could get a cheeseburger with fries and a milkshake.

Rollins and I always tried to be in the area at lunchtime. One day, as we sat down with our cheeseburgers, the actor Robert Stack and a very attractive woman came over to our table and asked if they could join us. (At that time, the television FBI series *The Untouchables* was very popular. Stack played the leading role of Elliot Ness.)

They had just arrived in-country and seemed very interested in knowing what was happening with the war and what Saigon was like. Rollins and I had never met a big-time Hollywood celebrity and were a bit tongue-tied. Answering their questions kept the conversation going, though. We had also not seen a Western woman (roundeye) in some time, which contributed to our awkwardness.

On another day, we had just left the Meyercord after having our cheeseburgers when the radio dispatcher informed us that a potential explosive had been reported there. We rushed back in and were led to a landing on the second-floor stairs. A wrapped parcel had been placed squarely in a corner.

I immediately ordered an evacuation of everyone in the hotel and had Rollins call the EOD team. Everyone was out in the street by the time the EOD team arrived. I led them to the landing and felt obligated to stay and watch as one of them used a jackknife to carefully open the parcel. Then they both started laughing hysterically…They had found two cheese sandwiches!

A week or so later while on patrol on the day shift there was an explosion on the jet-fuel pipeline feeding the Tan Son Nuht Airport on the edge of the city. The radio operator reported that we were the closest patrol to provide an escort for the EOD team, which was the same two guys from the Meyercord incident.

When we arrived, the Vietnamese Fire Department was getting the fire under control and were searching for a secondary explosive. We joined them in searching the pipeline. A cluster of dynamite was discovered, and we all ran to the spot. I hid behind a telephone pole while they calmly and expeditiously defused the explosive. When they finished, I stepped out from behind the pole, and one of them said, "Catch this!" and flipped a block of dynamite to me. I nearly peed my pants. I had never seen dynamite. It looked like a large bar of soap, and I thought dynamite was always volatile. Once again, they were highly amused.

An Army and Marine Joint Operation

When I first took up residence in the Victoria Hotel, I discovered that there was a full bar on the roof overlooking the whole city. There was a Vietnamese woman bartender on duty every night. You could see flares and hear bombs off in the distance while sipping your drink at the bar. The whole operation was privately run outside the military by a Sergeant Milson. I didn't like him. He was very cocky and patronizing toward me and other officers.

Milson was eventually arrested for violating currency regulations. The US military issued their own currency, called military pay currency, or MPC. He traded in MPC and Vietnamese dong and converted back to US dollars, which he secretly shipped back to the States.

After Milson was locked up, Marine Lieutenant Kemp approached me to see if I would help him keep the bar running. He probably had observed my affinity for bourbon and figured I had a lot to lose if the bar closed. He was right.

The first thing we did was to go to the PX and replenish the beer and booze inventory. We took up a collection from our fellow officers. We acquired temporary use of a truck from the MP motor pool, courtesy of my roommate. Kemp drove the truck and I rode in the truck bed in order to protect the cargo from street urchins. The bartender agreed to stay on.

The transition went smoothly. We eliminated Milson's markup and priced the drinks at cost. We obtained a movie screen and projector and showed a film every week under the stars. The bar was busy, and games of Liar's Dice were constantly in progress.

The Trans

Mrs. Tran, whom I initially had met in Long Binh through her laundry service, contacted me and invited me to her house for a family dinner. They lived within a well-kept collection of small homes near the Tan Son Nhat Airport. I think the homes were government housing for officers. There was an impressive topiary wall at the entrance. Major Tran was very friendly and worked as a propaganda officer. Their four boys were delightful and ranged in age from twelve to four.

The meal was very simple and tasty. We each received a bowl of rice. A platter of chicken and vegetables was passed around to top the rice. Nuoc mam (fish sauce) was the condiment. They showed me how to flip the ends of the chopsticks around so that when taking food from the platter you were not contaminating the food with the eating end of the chopsticks.

I was surprised to learn that they were not at all critical of Ho Chi Minh, the North Vietnamese leader. They said "Uncle Ho" was a nationalist at heart and wanted only one Vietnam. They too wanted a unified Vietnam. Regarding North Vietnam's relationship with Communist "Red" China, they pointed out that for hundreds of years the Vietnamese battled against Chinese attempts to take over their country and explained that the main thoroughfare in Saigon was named after the Trung sisters. These two sisters led a rebellion with an army of eighty thousand in AD 40, which expelled the Chinese emperor and his government. Some say they might be Chinese today if not for the Trungs.

The Tran family and I got together many times after that. They even invited me to attend a Sunday Mass with them at the Saigon Notre-Dame Cathedral. The Jesuits at BC were never able to convince me that there was a God, so I was willing to take the risk of a lightning strike by going into church.

The inside of the cathedral was magnificent. The ceremony was the same as all the Catholic churches I had attended. The church was packed full. When it was time to receive Communion, they rushed all at once to the Communion rail. Much to my amazement, they pushed and shoved one another, and no one appeared to be disturbed by this.

A couple of times I hosted the Trans at the "Club" Victoria for movie night, and we met for dinner every few weeks. At the end of my tour, they invited me to a going-away dinner at a restaurant near the airport. We ate outdoors, and when a couple of shots rang out behind me, I dove off my chair to the ground. It turned out to be a drunken Vietnamese soldier just shooting in the air. Evidently this was not unusual because no one made a fuss about it.

Saigon Cathedral

I think often about the Trans and wonder how they and their boys made out after our forces left Vietnam in 1975. Lists of Vietnamese refugees were published subsequently, and I checked every list that became available. Sandy and I agreed that if we found them, we would do all we could to help them resettle, even if it meant they temporarily moved in with us. We never had that opportunity.

Life on the Streets

A group of homeless kids hung out near my hotel. Like many kids throughout the city, they begged, stole, and did anything to survive. It was heartbreaking that they had nothing and nobody to care for them. They were smart and full of fun to be around.

If I was off duty and had some idle time, I would march them down the street to an open-air corner restaurant. After a good feed, we usually ordered sodas and moved to the foosball table. I am a bit of a game freak, but that game was new to me. It was not new to these kids; they beat me so badly I gave up and just watched them play.

We conversed in sign language, French, and pidgin English. An example: "good" was "number one," "bad" was "number ten," and "very bad" was "number fucken ten thousand." Also, "You *beaucoup sau*" meant "you are a big liar."

One day on patrol, I witnessed two Vietnamese Army soldiers walking hand in hand. I found out that it was customary for friends who were just friends to do this. I imagine many GIs took this the wrong way.

Another odd thing I began to notice in my travels around the city was that many of the poor people's mouths were colored red from chewing beetle nuts. This gave them a constant and mellow high, which I am sure helped them deal with their living conditions.

A Lesson Learned

The Saigon National Police (Canh Sat) wore white uniforms and were nicknamed the White Mice. They had a bad reputation with our MPs. It was rumored they were lazy, inept, and avoided patrolling parts of the city. Our battalion initiated a program whereby they would ride on patrols with our MPs. After a month or so, the feedback from the joint patrols was that the rumors about them were not far-fetched.

The Cholon District, known as Saigon Chinatown, included slums along the Saigon River canal. Families lived on small, dilapidated canal boats or in a maze of tiny shacks along the canal. The Viet Cong, labeled by us as "Charlie," were very active in this part of town, and it was an area the Saigon National Police shied away from.

House boats along canal in Cholon District

One night, we were slowly putting along the canal, when a scruffy-looking fellow jumped out of an alley and threw a grenade at us. Rollins saved our asses by jamming his foot on the gas pedal. The grenade went off just behind the jeep. I grabbed my M16 rifle from its holder on the dash and, in the process, shot holes in the canvas top of the jeep. I yelled at Rollins to stop and then I jumped out of the jeep in a purple rage. I ran back to the alley and proceeded to bust into shack after shack looking for the grenade guy. At a curve in the alley, I looked back and Rollins was right behind me.

"Goddammit it, Rollins, you should be back at the jeep monitoring the radio, not following me!"

He "yes sirred" me and left. I went a little farther down the alley and then headed back, realizing the idiocy of my behavior.

I had made myself a sitting duck for an ambush. I sheepishly got in the jeep and said very little, except to compliment Rollins on his quick reaction.

Later that night, on the other side of the city, we encountered four White Mice in the middle of the street. They had their pistols drawn on a US Army GI, who was brandishing a knife. They tended to be a little quick on the trigger, so I was worried.

As Rollins pulled us up next to them, I was grateful to see that the White Mice were backing off and that the GI was unharmed. As I approached him, it was clear that he was higher than a kite and not happy to see me. He was stumbling around, still wielding the knife.

I pushed him to the ground and pinned his arm with the knife to the street. I expected Rollins to jump in at any second. I glanced up to the jeep and saw him sitting behind the wheel with his arms crossed.

"Rollins! Get the fuck over here and help me with this clown!"

The GI passed out, and as we dragged him to the jeep, I asked Rollins why he didn't help right away.

"Well, sir, you said I was always to stay with the jeep to monitor the radio."

I learned from Rollins that if you ever want to screw your boss, just do exactly what you are told.

The anecdotal evidence I picked up, from troops returning from the field and from lower-level central command officers, led me to believe that our newly arrived Army and Marine infantry divisions were suffering heavy casualties. This was not in sync with press releases from Westmoreland's headquarters. It seemed as if in every reported battle, enemy losses were a multiple higher than ours. Earlier in the war, daily press briefings in Saigon had been dubbed the "Five O'clock Follies" by the war correspondents.

An infantry company was attached to our MP battalion. Their sole mission was to man static security posts. That meant they were in a cement kiosk in front of a building for twelve hours with a rifle and a radio, an extremely tedious and boring assignment, but it beat the hell out of being out in the jungle. When I was duty officer, I made a point of checking in with as many of these guard stations as I could, particularly the ones in the outlying areas of the city.

Late at night, in one of the most remote and sketchy areas, I found a guard sound asleep in his chair in the kiosk. I snuck around behind him and smacked him on the side of his helmet. My thought was that he was better off getting the shit scared out of him than being reported. This offense could warrant a transfer to the field and substantially decrease his odds of survival.

"What the hell would happen to you if I were the VC?" I shouted at him, and then told him I was not going to report him this time. He thanked me profusely.

Attacking your own men is against military regulations, and that was the second time I had been physical with a soldier. However, in this case I felt the end justified the means.

On another evening, we pulled into the MP station around midnight to check on things and get a coffee. A soldier in one of the cells was complaining loudly that he was in pain and needed help. I asked what his problem was, and one of the MPs piped up and said: "He was just drunk, sir, and raised one hell of a problem, so I handcuffed him and put him in the cell."

This was a bit unusual, so I went down the hall to his cell.

When I asked him what was wrong, he held up his hands and said the handcuffs were killing him. It was clear that the hand-cuffs had been put on way too tight. It would have been difficult to prove that the cuffs were intentionally put on too tight, but I had little doubt that they were.

I verbally emasculated the sadistic bastard who arrested him, and hopefully everyone in the station understood that using only the force necessary was what we did and that torture, however slight, was not what we did.

King Kong?

There is a small island in the Saigon River just outside the city. This was a relatively safe zone for American troops to relax, have a cookout, and play games. Conway and I figured out a day when my platoon, his motor-pool team, and an MP unit that guarded the Port of Saigon would be off duty. The MP guards provided steaks they had siphoned off a supply ship. Conway and I procured the beer and soda.

We all traveled to the island, followed by two trucks and a machine-gun jeep. It was a warm day and became warmer for Conway and me as we grilled all the steaks. To combat the heat, we consumed many cans of beer. This did not help our perfor-mance on the volleyball court.

We left the island ahead of the others and decided it would be fun to visit the Saigon Zoo. After wandering around the zoo, we were drawn to the gorilla exhibit. The secured cage area was surrounded by a cement wall with an iron railing on top. The gorilla started interacting with us by grunting and jumping around.

One of us had the bright idea that we could climb over the railing and get right next to the gorilla's cage. The gorilla seemed to like this and moved over next to the bars. We reached through the bars to touch him and he jumped back. He then climbed up on his roost and started hissing at us.

Conway was laughing his ass off until the gorilla swung down from his roost, reached through the bars, took his hat right off his head and brought it into the cage with him.

Conway was pissed and started wondering how the hell he could get his hat back. The gorilla was hanging on to the hat, so we tried to coax him back to the bars so we could grab it away. He came back to the bars waving the hat but kept it just out of reach.

I burst out laughing when the gorilla put the hat down and then peed all over it. The next thing I knew the gorilla went flying by the bars and whacked me soundly upside my head. Conway didn't get his hat back, and neither one of us got our sense of humor back for quite a while. The moral of this story is that sometimes animals can be more intelligent than humans.

Chapter 24

My Platoon

A squad of Australian MPs was assigned to my platoon. They were a bit older and more experienced than my men and wore the classic bush hats with the one side pinned up.

Platoons not on night duty took turns being on alert as a backup force. This entailed staying in the barracks and remaining sober. Periodically, I ran a practice drill and timed how long it took the platoon to assemble and be ready to board the trucks. One night, I caught wind of a beer party in progress and activated the call to duty.

I waited outside next to the trucks. In record time, the entire Aussie squad was assembled and in full gear. They looked sharp, and it was hard to tell they had been drinking.

About five minutes later, my disheveled platoon sergeant appeared. He did his best to hide the fact that he was totally cackled. In twos and threes, the rest of the platoon staggered in.

This was serious business. My punishment was to call the Alert Force to duty more often. I think they learned the lesson that trying to outdrink Aussies is a contest most Americans would never win.

A Show of Grace

A fellow MP officer, Ronald Akins, was promoted from second to first lieutenant. Several of his fellow MP lieutenants were invited to a "ceremony" at the Saigon officers' club. Custom required one to drink as much as one could to celebrate the grand event.

Ron was a Carolinian law school grad and was probably the smallest MP in the military. His size was fortunate for us, because we had to carry him the ten or so blocks back to our hotel. As we neared the hotel someone suggested that we have a nightcap in the small bar next to the hotel. Ron was sobering up a bit by then and thought this was a great idea. Three of us concurred. The place was full of GIs. We crammed into a small booth at the back of the bar.

Then we heard some commotion at the front of the bar. There was an eleven o'clock curfew on all bars in the city. This was enforced by the MPs, who happened to be coming through the front door…That was when I remembered that my platoon was on duty that night.

Ron decided to walk right out the front door, and the rest of us tried to escape out the back. I had almost made it to the men's room when two large hands landed on my shoulders. I was spun around and faced the very large and efficient Private Jones from my own platoon.

"Well, good evening, sir," he said.

"Jones, if you don't mind, I'll just stay out here."

"No problem, sir. Have a good evening," he replied.

Ron told me the next day that he just walked right out the front door, complimenting the men on the way for doing a good job. Over the next few days, there was a lot of quiet snickering when I walked around my platoon's barracks. Not penalizing my platoon for the Alert Force fiasco turned out to be a good idea in that it may have helped me not get arrested by my own men.

My Views

After six months in-country, I was convinced that our government had made a big mistake in fighting this war. There were several reasons.

The Trans' information about the hostile relationship of Vietnam and China over hundreds of years convinced me that although the Chinese were helping the North Vietnamese, they would always be their enemy. The Trans were from the industrial North and explained the economic problems caused by an industrial North separated from an agricultural South, which reminded me of the similar economic issues in our own country's Civil War. The morale of the general citizenry was low, evidenced by the continual demonstrations against the South Vietnamese government, including the self-immolation by Buddhist monks. My experience with a totally unmotivated and inept National Police force compared to the dogged determination of the enemy was convincing. Finally, it was their civil war, but the United States was directly fighting the war for them instead of maintaining a secondary support role.

In a letter to Papa before he died, I wrote that unless we put a soldier on every square foot of Vietnamese soil, we would never win the war. His return letter surprised me, because it was the opposite of his gruff persona. He mentioned how difficult the separation from the family is and how demoralizing and frustrating it must be to fight in war you don't believe in. He signed off, uncharacteristically, with "Love Papa."

The Liar

My mother wrote that my brother Denny's good friend Billy, son of the Currans who lived upstairs from us in Mattapan, had recently arrived in Vietnam. I planned to find out what unit he was with and make contact with him.

Then another letter came from my mother several weeks later. Billy had been killed in combat serving in an Army infantry unit.

I wanted so much to be of some small comfort to Billy's parents and let them know his death was not in vain. But goddammit, I did not feel this was true.

However, if they believed in the war and that Billy died for a good cause, a reinforcement of that belief coming from me might help them in their grief. In my letter of condolence to them, I lied and extolled the virtues of our country's commitment to the people of South Vietnam in their fight to stay free from North Vietnam.

Counselor

When my men were on duty, they were usually under the "operational control" of another officer. MPs were often used on temporary assignments to other units. Some of my men volunteered for extra duty as gunners on helicopters.

Because of this setup, I went out of my way to maintain open and frequent communications. I encouraged them to drop by my office anytime without notice, and they did. Some of the meet-

ings required the skill sets of a chaplain, a coach, or a bartender.

One day, Specialist Four Jaworski came into my office, and the first thing he said was that his wife was pregnant.

"Congratulations!" I exclaimed.

"Sir, I have been over here for ten months."

He was almost in tears, and I was at a loss for words. I finally got him talking about the history of his relationship with his wife. All I could do was listen and commiserate. I think he sought me out because he was reluctant to talk to his buddies.

The most memorable meeting I had was with Specialist Four Goodman. "Sir, I am going crazy! I don't believe that we should be fighting over here and yet I want to do my job. What the hell should I do?"

"It's been driving me crazy also, Goodman," I said. "Here is how I handle it. It's like in a football game when we were told to never stop playing until the whistle is blown. If you stand around looking, someone will likely take you down."

I think he got my point. Then he asked me what to do if he had to kill someone. I told him that was his job and a slight hesitation could prevent him from ever seeing his family again. As far as I could tell, he performed his duties very well and was a good MP.

My views of my country's participation in this war had no effect on my own job performance, which at its most basic level was to kill or be killed.

Chapter 25

High and Low Anxiety

It was after midnight when the desk sergeant radioed me that they had a lieutenant in custody for the misappropriation of a vehicle and being under the influence. Whenever an officer committed an infraction, the duty officer was involved as soon as possible. I asked how he behaved, and the report from the arresting MP was that he was friendly and not a problem.

I returned to the MP station, and much to my astonishment, Brady, a fellow I played football with at La Salle, was sitting in a chair across from the front desk. He was very repentant and explained that he'd had a few and then borrowed a jeep from another unit to go to a bar. We had a great time catching up. He was in Army intelligence and bored to death working in an air-conditioned office studying the latest enemy weaponry. I was jealous of his work environment.

I explained to him that in the military, misbehavior or violations were handled first by his commanding officer. I said that I would keep the incident off the police blotter and would not inform his CO. I brought him back to his unit and emphasized to him that the "luck of the Irish" might not be there in the future.

Another time, the dispatcher asked if I could quickly get over to the PX (post exchange–military department/grocery store). He said two MPs were being bullied by an Army major. When I arrived, the two MPs and the major were at the entrance. The MPs appeared to be blocking him from entering.

Their job was to check everyone's IDs and direct them to leave their weapons at the door. The major had refused to do either and had been demanding they get out of his way. He claimed they were disobeying a direct order.

I got right in the major's face and said in a very loud voice that he should be ashamed of himself for trying to prevent these two soldiers from doing their duty and that superior rank or not, I would take his ass down to the MP station and book him for conduct unbecoming an officer and abuse of enlisted men. He turned red in the face and left the building.

In the dead of night, a patrol requested my assistance because they had come across a totally naked American who was found lying by the side of the road and claimed he was a colonel. I couldn't get any more information out of him when I arrived, since he was drifting in and out of consciousness—too drunk to speak. My driver and I crammed him into the back seat of our jeep and brought him to the hospital. I wondered later if he really was a colonel.

MPs often had to deal with American civilians other than the press. I was at the MP station when two civilians were brought in. They had been arrested for some kind of obnoxious behavior in a bar. They were still being obstreperous and insisted that we had no jurisdiction over them. They said they were pilots for Air

America and cockily presented their IDs to me. I told them that I was not a judge or a lawyer and that they would be spending the night with us. I left instructions not to press charges and to just kick them out in the morning. I heard later that Air America had some kind of connection with our CIA.

On Stage

I was and still am mechanically challenged. Nevertheless, I was given the temporary assignment of reviewing the condition and maintenance procedures of the jeeps in the battalion motor pool. Conway was back home by then. When I showed up, I was greeted by Sergeant Adams. I immediately confessed my total ignorance of moving metal parts. We chatted as he patiently showed me how to perform an inspection on a jeep.

Our common interest in music came up. I told him I was a drummer and about my rock and jazz experiences. He was a guitarist, and when off duty, he actually played in a Vietnamese band. He said that their drummer was horrible, and it would be fun if I came by and sat in one night.

A week or two later I showed up at the nightclub. The band was playing when I arrived. Adams was right; the drummer was bad. He seemed half asleep and was way behind the beat with no dynamics. Adams invited me up to play the next set.

I remember we played "Mustang Sally," "Susie Q," and a couple of other songs. I couldn't believe it—there I was in a war zone having great fun in a Vietnamese rock band. Adams hoped that maybe my appearance would inspire his drummer to show signs of life.

I still have trouble believing that I played in a rock 'n' roll band in a war zone.

Carnage

Rollins had been promoted and my new driver, Clark, was a serious, all-business type from Massachusetts. On night patrols, we listened to Armed Forces Radio on a small transistor radio. We also had buzzing from the two rather large military radios mounted in the back of the jeep.

It had been a quiet evening filled with some fine Motown tunes. As dawn was breaking, the radios started crackling with units reporting in. The night dispatcher told me that a Vietnamese battalion convoy in the vicinity of General Westmoreland's headquarters was under attack.

We were not far away. I could hear what sounded like mortar rounds one after another. Impossible, I thought. We were in the middle of the city. I ordered the patrols to stay in their districts except for the machine-gun jeeps. A common VC ploy was to draw us into one area and then they would attack another.

The shelling had stopped as we pulled up on a side street. I jumped out of the jeep and ran around the corner, nearly stepping on a severed hand. "Carnage" is the only word to describe the scene. Smoke was billowing up all around me, and ammunition from the trucks was popping off. Burned and bloody bodies were all over the place. A few of our patrols had also just arrived. I instructed them to cordon off the streets and clear the way for the emergency vehicles. Saigon Fire Department trucks and personnel were pouring in. They concentrated on tending to the wounded and working to get them on stretchers for evacuation.

I came across a US Special Forces major (Green Beret) in the middle of the mess. An American reporter had a mic in his face and another American newsman had a camera on the two of them.

The major had had enough of the obnoxious interviewer and was about to belt him when I got between the two of them and pulled him away. I confronted the reporter and told him to get the hell out of the area for his own safety.

He got in my face with his mic and started ranting about freedom of the press. He said he was not going anywhere. I smelled booze on his breath as I grabbed him and spun him around to give him the bum's rush out of there. The camera was still rolling as we struggled. Two of my men quickly moved in and grabbed hold of him. He was kicking and yelling as they dragged him away.

The major stood there with tears of anguish running down his face. He told me he had spent months training and working closely with the men in this infantry battalion. He added that they were just passing through the city to their first deployment.

When we got back to the MP station, I learned that the VC had removed the roof of a house in a marketplace to fire the mortars. They left behind a timing device on an explosive, which killed a Vietnamese policeman and a small child and injured thirty others. The next day I learned that sixteen soldiers died and forty were wounded in the Vietnamese battalion.

I returned to my hotel after filing my report. I was shaken by the whole thing and went to the bar on the roof to have break-fast with my bourbon buddy, Mr. Jim Beam. After a few drinks, I got word that the headquarters' area general wanted to see me immediately.

I kept it all together as I reported in to the Saigon headquarters general with a crisp salute. It was just like a scene from a WWII or Korean War film, where the protagonist violates a military regulation or command and his superior says to the soldier, "I don't know whether to court-martial or promote you."

The general said, "I have received a complaint from"— (whatever network it was)—"news agency about your behavior this morning. I have to tell you, Lieutenant, I would have done the same thing you did. I'll handle this. Not to worry. Now get out of here."

The next evening when I went on duty, I was informed that a reporter from that news show would be riding with me the whole night to see how we operated. Yes, it was that same jerk doing his penance. He was quietly pouting the whole time. I really enjoyed that evening.

My mother wrote that I was on an evening news show that covered the incident. Not exactly the fifteen minutes of fame I would have chosen.

R & R

After a certain amount of time in-country, every soldier was eligible for seven days of rest and relaxation. When your orders came through, you were pulled from whatever you were doing, told to don civilian clothes, and put on a plane to the destination of your choice. Most of the large cities in South East Asia, Australia, and Hawaii were on the list. I chose the least popular destination because I wanted to get as far away as possible from other military personnel. There were only three of us on the commercial flight to Penang, Malaysia. We just nodded to each other on our trip, and I rarely saw them at our destination.

I negotiated a deal with a Malaysian motorized trishaw driver to be my full-time guide and transportation for five days. By using hand signals, I tried to communicate to him that I wanted to have a lobster dinner. Looking for a New England lobster meal in the tropical Far East was a weird manifestation of my longing to be home. He understood that I wanted to have dinner.

At the first restaurant, he watched me talking to the maître d' while flailing with my arms and hands in my attempt to imitate a lobster. He interceded and told me that whatever the hell I wanted, they did not have it.

At the next restaurant, they seemed to understand me. As I was being seated, I looked for my driver to follow us to the table, but he was out of sight. I had assumed that he would join me for dinner but was told this was not allowed. I protested mildly but respected their culture, and I was starving. Instead of lobster, I was served a plate of the largest prawns I had ever seen. They were fresh, tender, and delicious.

The next day I took a bus from the city to a beach-side hotel. Penang had been part of the British Empire and this hotel showed it. Linen-covered tables with real silverware were spread among the shady trees alongside the beach. I ordered a bottle of wine with lunch, and afterward stayed seated, enjoying the wine.

The sea was calm and inviting, and I wondered why no one was swimming. I decided to be the first and must have spent an hour in the warm water, floating around on my back. When I returned to the table to finish the wine, I asked the waiter why nobody else was in the water. He told me it was the season for very poisonous sea snakes.

My driver was an amusing fellow, and touring the city in a trishaw was enjoyable. I was able to have him join me for lunch and dinner in the less fancy places. Every day I slept late, had lunch, did some touring, and then headed for a bar.

One afternoon, I entered a place with a horseshoe-shaped bar. On one side of the bar were several white English soldiers, and on the other sat a large black English soldier. I sat down next to him and introduced myself. He told me he was from Fiji and had been in the bar for a while. After a few drinks, we headed off to an open-air Indian restaurant for dinner.

We ordered chicken curry and beer, which came in very large bottles. He plucked the chicken out of the curry and ate it with his hands. We both sopped up the curry sauce with bread. After he had eaten most of the meat off the bones, he sucked them clean and went after the marrow. Then I remembered that the Fiji islanders had been cannibals. I couldn't help picturing his great-grandfather gnawing away on a bone off a New Bedford whaler who might have strayed too far into the jungle.

We ordered more curry and beer, then just more beer. He began slurring his words and was having trouble staying in his chair. A Malaysian Army major had been sitting by himself at the table next to us. I invited him to join our beer fest. The major and I became involved in an animated conversation on how to deal with guerrilla warfare. The British and the Malaysians had recently subdued the uprising by the Malaysian Chinese, who were Communists.

The Fijian passed out with his head on the table. The major said that all British soldiers were on an eleven o'clock curfew and that we should get him to his barracks. He summoned a taxi, and we somehow managed to stuff our friend into it. The major prepaid the driver and we returned to our table.

The sun was coming up as we finished our last beer. He wished me continued luck in Vietnam. The next day I was anxious to get back to my unit and finish my tour of duty.

Chapter 26

Getting Short

*T*he military has independent legal procedures that are detailed in the Uniform Code of Military Justice. There are three levels of court-martial: summary, special, and general. Summary court-martial is for minor violations, which are handled by a commanding officer or military lawyer. It has very limited punishment levels—loss of pay, demotion, or restrictions. A special court-martial is the intermediate court level. It consists of a military judge, trial counsel (prosecutor), defense counsel, and a minimum of three officers sitting as a panel of court members, or jury. An enlisted accused may request a court hearing composed of at least one-third enlisted personnel. A general court-martial is for major crimes and offenses.

Any officer in a command can be called upon to serve as defense counsel. I don't know what process is used to decide who is chosen, but I was assigned to defend a soldier subject to a special court-martial, where the maximum penalty was a year in prison, forfeiture of twelve months' pay, and a dishonorable discharge.

My "client" was an Army private who'd deserted his unit and was apprehended while pushing a pedicab in Saigon. He wore the standard outfit of a pedicab driver—pajama-like black shirt and pants and a large straw hat—and had been living undercover for more than a year.

He was in the prison at Long Binh base camp. I had arrived at Long Binh eleven months earlier, and this was my first return. During my time there, it was a dirt pile with a collection of tents and one headquarters building. In the short time since, it had been transformed into a small city with permanent buildings. One of those was the prison, or stockade.

I checked in with the CO of the stockade. He said my client, Peter, was to be tried by a special court-martial, but technically he could have been tried by a general court-martial for desertion. He qualified as a deserter because he had been AWOL for more than thirty days and seemed to have no intention of returning. The maximum sentence for desertion was life in prison, or execution. Since WWII, there had been no executions, and the military rarely sought convictions for desertions. When they did, prison times were greatly reduced from the maximum.

I interviewed Peter in a small room with a table and three small chairs. It looked like the typical interrogation rooms you see on the police television shows. Since his guilt or innocence was not in question, my job was to work on possible mitigating circumstances to get a reduced sentence.

I spent several hours with him. Peter was the only son of an Army colonel. He had grown up constantly moving from place to place, as many military kids do. He was very shy and the last thing he ever wanted was to have a career in the Army. His father, on the other hand, had great plans for him in the Army. This clash led Peter to leave home after high school. He was then swept up in the draft. He had other problems, too, but I felt like the relationship with his father should be the mitigating factor. I visited him a couple more times before the trial.

At the trial I was a nervous wreck because I had the sole responsibility of ensuring that Peter got a fair trial. I could hardly hold a pencil in my hand to take notes. When I rose to present my case, my heart was doing double time and my mouth went dry. After I squeaked out a few words, I found my groove and got into my defense.

Peter was sentenced to five months in prison and forfeiture of five months' pay. I congratulated myself for winning Peter a significant reduction from the maximum penalty and avoiding a dishonorable discharge. Then I wondered how many of the career officers on the jury were swayed toward a lenient sentence due to their having their own problems with their own children or had learned of problems in other families brought on by family life in the military.

How Short Are You?

All Army personnel were required to serve no more than twelve months in Vietnam. If you were nearing your departure date, you were said to be "short." A common question was "How short are you?" Many short-timers came up with creative analogies such as: "I am so short I couldn't climb on top of a box of matches."

Some soldiers had calendars tracking the exact number of days they had left. Some of these calendars had the number of days shown on an outline of a female form. That is all I will say about that.

If you had one hundred days left to serve, you were a double-digit midget because one hundred days was ninety-nine days plus a "wake-up." Ten days or less made you a single-digit midget.

I came across a "single-digit midget" in the course of responding to a terrorist attack on an isolated government building. He was alone and crouched by the side of another building some distance from the action. "What the hell are you doing back here, soldier?" I barked.

"Sir, I have only two days left, sir!"

"Stay here and have a safe trip home," I said.

"Thank you, sir," he replied.

A Tragedy

When I became so short that I could walk under a jeep without banging my head, I was introduced to my replacement, Second Lieutenant Leonard Martin. He had just arrived in-country and had come directly from MP school. He appeared to be quiet and very laid-back. At first I thought he was the cool, silent type.

After he rode with us for a week, he seemed to be disinterested in what I was telling him and never asked any questions. He even fell asleep in the back of the jeep a couple of times. Not much was going on in the city that week, and maybe that was why he didn't take interest in the job. Or maybe he was that bad combination of stupid and cocky.

In the course of briefing him on the Alert Force, I told him there was often trouble at Tan Sun Nhat Airbase just outside the city. On the way to the base, there was a major time-saving shortcut. It was a narrow, alley-like street bordered by buildings. It was a street that was perfect for an ambush by hostile forces. I emphasized what my trainer had told me: *never* lead the Alert Force through the alley!

I had been stationed back in the States for five months when I received word that during the January Tet Offensive, he had led the Alert Force's trucks into the "alley." The Viet Cong had sealed off the end of the street and ambushed the Alert Force. I was beside myself with grief for my men and furious at the gross incompetence and neglect of the sorry son of a bitch who led them into harm's way. I heard he was wounded and may have died. I never cared to find out what happened to him.

Per the Army publication the *Guidon*, "Sixteen MPs were killed in an ambush as they responded to a reported attack on an officers' quarters near Tan Son Nuht Airport. In all, the 716th MP Battalion suffered 27 killed and 44 wounded during the Tet Offensive."

A Very Careless Departure

The Army tried to station soldiers returning from Vietnam near their homes but were not always successful. I was elated to find out that I would be stationed at Fort Devens, where my Army career started. I was also relieved because the standard joke was if you want to live in Massachusetts, request California.

I couldn't believe that I would be going home in a week. I had the same feeling of anticipation like a kid at Christmas, getting a bicycle, getting a driver's license, or kissing a girl. But I was convinced it was not going to happen and thought that subconsciously I tried to ensure it wouldn't. Or maybe this is all self-serving bullshit for my bad behavior as a single-digit midget with three days and a wake-up left.

With little left to do, I decided that it would be nice to check on Peter, the prison inmate. I signed out a jeep in the afternoon and drove alone up to Long Binh. He was in good spirits and we had a long conversation about his future and what he would do with his life when he got back to the States.

It was late afternoon, and I decided to get a couple of drinks at the Vietnam officers' club in nearby Bien Hoa. I checked my pistol at the door and headed for the bar. The bourbon was going down easily, and I decided to stay for dinner. The band started up as I finished eating and they were playing some good tunes.

I drove out of town to get back onto Route 1 to Saigon. While trying to turn onto the ramp to the highway, I evidently did not notice the stopped truck in front of me.

Things got very fuzzy after that. I remember the guys in the truck trying to help me bend the front fender enough so that the tires would turn. The next thing I knew, I was in the motor pool of my old unit the 552nd and was watching the guys working on the front end of the jeep.

I was warmly received, and they told me that the jeep looked a lot better now, but the signs of an accident were quite apparent. I thanked them profusely, and in the middle of the night, I headed back down Route 1. Nobody was on the road and, thankfully, that included the Viet Cong. I drove very fast and drove even faster when I realized my pistol was still at the Vietnam officers' club.

When I arrived at our motor pool, I explained the whole mess to the night crew. They said they would hide the jeep until I left.

The next day the supply sergeant graciously agreed to sign me off as having turned in my equipment and my weapons.

I boarded a chartered commercial plane at Tan Son Nhut. What a feeling of freedom I felt as the plane lurched sharply into the air! I felt eternally grateful to all the guys who helped me through my self-induced crisis. Any one of them could have turned me in and I might have ended up with Peter in stockade.

Chapter 27

Stateside

We were about an hour away from landing in San Francisco when the fight began. How it started I will never know. Was it one of the flight attendants or a rowdy GI? I became involved when a pillow hit me squarely in the face. I joined the fight and hummed it back, hitting a crew member. She was busy launching one back at another crew member. It was on! The laughter was infectious. Pillows were flying everywhere. Panic struck me when the fight shifted everyone to one side of the plane. I envisioned the head-line: PLANE RETURNING FROM VIETNAM CRASHES IN THE OCEAN DUE TO IMBALANCE CAUSED BY PILLOW FIGHT.

Fuck You for Your Service

We landed safely and, to a man, stepped lively with smiles on our faces as we hurried off the plane and crossed the runway. One soldier fell to his knees to kiss the ground. I was happily strolling through the airport on the way to my connecting flight, when a colorful group of long-haired men and braless long-haired women approached me. They blocked my way and started yelling at me.

"Baby killer" was the worst insult. Their leader got in my face. He probably wanted me to take a swing at him. Instead, I loudly asked the group: "Why the hell are you picking on me? Take it up with the president and your congressmen. Tell me why, you morons!"

The Reunion

The flight to Boston had a stopover in Chicago. An Army sergeant had a window seat next to me. He nudged me and said, "Holy Cow, Lieutenant! Ted Williams is boarding the plane." I confirmed his report when I saw Ted getting into his seat in first class. The sergeant and I chatted on our way to Boston on how great a baseball player Ted had been and that he was a childhood hero of ours.

At Boston's Logan Airport, I stood in front of the carousel baggage claim in a state of high anxiety. I had hardly slept in forty-eight hours. I was strung out by the anticipation of seeing Sandy with our two babies, Dylan and Eric.

I felt a tap on my shoulder. "Are you coming or going?" It was Ted Williams!

I was tongue-tied and had to think hard about whether I was coming or going. "I'm c-c-coming," I stuttered.

"Do they have any snakes over there?" he asked.

"Yes, yes, big snakes, big snakes," I replied.

"We didn't have any snakes in Korea," he said.

The Red Sox were in the playoffs for first time in many years, and I asked him if that was why he was in Boston. "No," he replied. "I'm headed to my baseball camp." A skycap approached to inform Ted that his luggage was ready. Ted wished me good luck as he left.

I then caught sight of Sandy heading toward me. She was

holding Eric. Dylan was walking and holding Sandy's free hand. Caught in a sudden time warp, I thought Eric was Dylan and wondered who that older kid was.

I snapped out of it and ran toward them. Everything seemed to be in slow motion. When I reached Sandy, I blurted out… "Guess who I just met!"

Decompressing

I had two weeks' leave before reporting to Fort Devens. My parents loaned us the use of their cottage on Horseneck Beach.

There was a cool autumn northwest wind blowing my first day on the beach. Sandy was back at the cottage with the boys. Underneath my feelings of happiness and gratitude that I made it home lurked a sense of dread that things were going too well and something bad would happen. When I returned to the cottage, I was depressed and irritable.

This attitude would come and go. Many ordinary things that were important to most people were insignificant to me. If we forgot to put out the trash, so what? Nobody was hurt, were they?

Sandy and I were working through the process of becoming reacquainted. A year's absence makes a big difference. She had routines for running the household and caring for the boys. I didn't have any routines and found myself getting in her way. What I thought were helpful suggestions, she interpreted as giving orders. The solution to this problem was obvious. I backed away and directed my energy toward entertaining my sons. I held them and fed them, read stories, and crawled around on the floor playing with them.

Chapter 28

Fort Devens—Again

With six months left of active duty, I was placed in charge of the MP company that provided the police and security for the base at Fort Devens. I reported to the provost marshal (Army for chief of police) who was an MP major. He reported to the post general. The major was also responsible for the New England Stockade (prison).

Junior officers with families were housed in cozy duplexes on the base. The commissary and officers' club were minutes away. A cardiologist and his wife lived next door to us.

For the most part, it was easy duty, consisting of all the normal police procedures you read about, but with squad cars instead of the jeeps we had in Vietnam. The well-seasoned noncommissioned officers ran everything. I drank a lot of coffee and read newspapers and magazines. Traffic violations, drunken altercations, and domestic disturbances composed the majority of the workload.

Zorba

My mother-in-law's dachshund died. When she came to visit, we presented her with a basset hound puppy. When she leaned over to pet him, he bit her on the lip, immediately ending their relationship.

We kept the puppy and sarcastically named him Zorba. The vet said Zorba had rickets from having been maltreated by the breeder. I stopped payment on the $50 check I had written to purchase him. When the breeder called me to demand a cash payment, I told him Zorba had rickets and chastised him for his total neglect of his dogs. I threatened to report him to the Humane Society.

Sergeant Jones was the company first sergeant and was very close to retirement. With his jovial way and physique, he would have made a great Santa Claus.

He informed me that Private Tasca, a scraggily looking fellow who worked in the motor pool, was in trouble. It seems when Tasca returned from Vietnam, he rented a car for a few days but drove it for three weeks and then abandoned it.

We met with Tasca and he explained that the rental car company was threatening him with larceny. I contacted the company and, over the next two days, tried to negotiate a payment plan. The problem was getting them to agree to a long payment plan that Tasca could realistically afford, which was very little. Finally, they said that they would try to get approval from headquarters, but they were not very hopeful.

Two weeks later I received a letter that requested my appearance in Lowell District Court in regard to a larceny.

I summoned my newly arrived executive officer, Lieutenant Cianci, who was a Villanova Law School grad from Providence. He had taken Tasca under his wing as his driver. I asked him if he would be willing to defend Tasca in court.

He jumped at the idea and suggested we immediately summon Tasca. We met with Tasca and Sergeant Jones. Cianci told Tasca to get his uniform pressed and get a haircut. Tasca had not acquired any service medals in Vietnam. Cianci convinced Jones to lend Tasca his vast array of combat, airborne, and service medals.

Tasca drove the squad car on our trip to court in Lowell. Cianci and I sat in back wearing our MP brassards on the sleeves of our green dress uniforms. When we approached the courthouse, Cianci insisted Tasca turn on the flashing light on top of the car. He also insisted we park in the no-parking area right in front of the courthouse steps.

Heads turned as we approached the clerk of the court. "Good morning. I am Lieutenant Dobbyn, here on behalf of Private Tasca."

He searched the register. "I don't have a Tasca here. What is your name again?"

"Dobbyn," I replied.

"Ah yes. Here it is. Dobbyn…larceny of a dog."

When Cianci realized what was happening, he doubled over, laughing. Murmurs spread throughout the court, interspersed with more laughter.

I looked around the room and spotted the sleazeball who had sold me Zorba. When we went before the judge, he ordered the breeder and his shiny-pants lawyer and me to come to an agreement. Cianci and I went to a meeting room off the court-room. I told him that I was not going to compromise because the sleazeball was the guilty one, not me. Cianci went back and forth between his lawyer and me. He got them down to $40, but I reiterated that the breeder should be in jail for cruelty to animals and that I would not pay a dime. We finally settled at $25 after Cianci convinced me that in the eyes of the law I was guilty. He knew I had been interviewing with a couple of certified public accounting firms for a job after my service, and he reminded me I would never be hired as a CPA with that on my record.

We had to find a home for Zorba because he bit Eric on the cheek when they were playing together on the floor. It was the pain from the rickets. Luckily, a woman who lived on a farm in Maine agreed to take him, even after we explained the ricket complications.

After the Army, Buddy Cianci went on to serve as the mayor of Providence for many years. He was very popular and did a lot of good work improving the city. He eventually got in trouble with the law, though, and in 2002 went to prison for five years.

After his release, he was a radio talk show host for WPRO in Providence. He also published his memoir, *Pasta and Politics*. My stepfather, Joe, went to one of his signings for the book and mentioned I was his son and that I was vacationing in Rhode Island. Buddy gave my father his contact information, which led to us meeting for dinner in Federal Hill, the Italian section of Providence.

It had been about forty years since we'd last met. I reminded him that I was his first client when he defended me in the dog larceny case. I was a little disappointed when said he did not recall any of that, which to me was an unforgettable incident in my life. During dinner several people stopped by our table to thank Buddy for helping them.

The New Warden

I was summoned to the provost marshal's office. I had seen very little of the shifty, smooth-talking major, and that was fine with me. He told me I was reassigned to the base's New England Confinement Facility (stockade) as the confinement officer, known as the warden in civilian life. He also said that the Army was short of MP captains, and if I served for an additional three months or more as the confinement officer, I would be promoted to captain. I had three months left and no prospects of employment, so I signed on, extending my duty to six months.

Sergeant Chevalier (Sarge), from Rhode Island, ran the stockade. He was an E8, the second-highest enlisted rank. He had worked primarily in confinement his whole Army career.

The first thing he told me was that the stockade was grossly overcrowded. We had more than two hundred inmates, which was twice the amount it was designed to hold. The second thing he said was that many of the prisoners believed that they did not belong in prison and they would request to see me to plead their cases. He suggested that meeting with them would be a waste of time. I was not sure what I could do if I thought one of them was innocent, but felt they needed to be listened to. Many hours were spent listening to their stories and never was there any reason for me to believe that they did not belong in confinement.

There was constant unrest and problems due to the tight quarters. Sarge informed me of a prisoners' fund with a couple of hundred dollars in it that had not been tapped for some time. I got the brilliant idea that making games available would keep the prisoners busy and reduce the high number of altercations. He strongly advised me against doing that. Once again, I ignored his advice. A bloodletting, vicious fight broke out over a Monopoly game, and within two days all the games were destroyed, with their pieces thrown everywhere.

After seeing that I was not bringing anything worthwhile to the table to improve prisoners' morale and operational conditions, I sat back and, for the most part, let Sarge do his thing.

The majority of the inhabitants in the stockade were AWOLS (absent without leave). There were a few serious offenders held in detention before trial, and the rest were guilty of misdemeanors such as assault and theft. Prisoners earned one of four custody levels: trustee, minimum, medium, and maximum. Very bad behavior could result in solitary confinement. Minimum-security prisoners were sent out on work details, escorted by guards with shotguns.

The Rabbit

William Furbush was a gentle and likable nineteen-year-old. He was an AWOL serving a short sentence in minimum custody and was usually well behaved. The only problem was that whenever he got outside on a work detail, he would make a run for it. The "Rabbit" was hard to catch.

I really felt bad for him because I believed he was a good soul, but he was disturbed. After his latest escape attempt, I decided to get personally involved to help him. We spent many hours together. He mentioned his mother all the time. When his mother came to visit, she struck me as the controlling type, and I theorized that maybe the Rabbit was overly dependent on her.

The Rabbit convinced me he would not run again. He went back on guarded work detail and behaved beautifully. I congratulated him and told him that if he continued to behave, we would make him a trustee—meaning no armed guards.

I told Sarge about this and he laughed. "Once a runner always a runner! Good luck with that one, sir."

I decided to give the Rabbit a little test to prove Sarge wrong. I asked the guards to bring Rabbit to meet me at the front gate. I told them we were going outside for a walk and that I was taking full responsibility for his custody.

In the midst of having a lovely chat, he ran like hell for the woods. One of the patrols picked him up in no time.

It was just a few days later that his mother visited again. She didn't ask to meet me. Over the next few days, the guards reported that the Rabbit was depressed one minute and happy the next.

A phone call woke me around midnight. The Rabbit was in the hospital. He had cut off his ear and handed it to one of the guards. They brought the ear with them to the post hospital for an attempt to sew it back on.

The operation was a success. When I visited him, he had a protective cuff over his ear and was in good spirits. I cautioned the guard at the door to be ready for his next run. Later, he did make a run for it and was tackled in the hallway. He banged his ear when he fell and lost it permanently.

Extracurricular Activities

The post commanding general insisted that all of his staff and the staff of his staff could not go off-duty until he went home. His sergeant major would call to let us know when we were to be released. At five o'clock, we left a window open so we could hear the phone and went outside to play horseshoes. I became quite good at this game because the call from the general rarely came before six. Eventually, we began to sneak out during the day to play.

Sarge talked about golf a lot and volunteered to take me out on the base golf course to learn the game. I was a little nervous about sneaking out while on duty, but he explained that if someone of importance were trying to reach us, he would get the office to call an MP patrol to drive out onto the course and pick us up. They would have a pretty good idea of what hole we were on because we would pass a few MP stations on our round. Because Sarge was near retirement and I was on my way out of the Army, we played quite often while on duty.

The driver of the squad car that raced up behind us on the front nine yelled out that the general wanted to see me immediately. We threw our clubs in the trunk and jumped in. When we reached the office, I changed quickly into my uniform and the driver raced me over to the headquarters building.

Saved again by loyal MPs.

What a Riot

I received a call in the middle of the night that several prisoners had escaped. I knew we were not exactly Alcatraz or Fort Leavenworth, but their escape method was a classic: they tied bedsheets together and went out the second-floor window. My immediate response was "You cannot be serious!"

The next morning, I learned that the escapees were all AWOLs from the large room that was jammed with bunk beds. All but two of the escapees had been picked up on the base by our patrols. The others were captured in a couple of days. The procedure, which I was told rarely failed, was to send two MPs to their home. One rang the front doorbell and the other caught the escapee running out the back door.

Later, I received another evening phone call. It seems the prisoners were beginning to riot. I arrived on the scene around 2200 hours (10:00 p.m.). The riot was in full progress. Mattresses had been set on fire. Sinks and toilets were being ripped up and smashed against the windows. I thought I was in a replay of the film *Riot in Cell Block 11*. Sarge handed me the megaphone.

"What do you want me to say?" I asked him.

"Just tell them to stop immediately or we will be coming in with tear gas."

"Okay, okay, got it," I replied. I turned on the megaphone. "Attention, attention, this is Captain Dobbyn. I order you to stop everything immediately or we will come in with tear gas." I repeated this three times. If anything, the intensity level of the riot increased.

He handed me a gas mask and said, "You lead, sir, and I will be right behind you."

When the tear gas was fired, I rushed in with Sarge on my heels, followed by the rest of the troops. There was no resistance, and everyone and everything was brought under control very quickly.

The next morning, we met for cleanup and a recovery plan. I asked how fast we could get the broken windows repaired. It was March and pretty nippy out. Sarge said there was no rush to do that. "Let them freeze their asses off for a while. It will make them think twice before they act up again." I agreed, particularly since we had decided not to press charges because it would be too difficult to sort out the instigators from the innocent.

I recently learned that in this same time period, the confinement facilities at Fort Jackson, South Carolina, Fort

Leavenworth, Kansas, and Long Binh, Vietnam, also had major riots. Anti-war sentiment, overcrowding, inexperienced guard forces, and racial tensions were cited as the major causes.

Lying Low

In June 1968, I had only a couple of weeks left before my discharge. I had landed a job in the Boston office of Price Waterhouse, a large public accounting firm. I never wanted to be an accountant, but I knew that as an auditor, I could work in many different companies and learn how the business world operated. The other reason I accepted was that I didn't have any other prospects for employment.

Sandy and I had just started the process of buying a house. I had turned over all of my military responsibilities to others and was just ticking off the days on the calendar. I was stunned and horrified to learn that while the work-detail guards were entering their barracks, one of them dropped his shotgun and it went off, killing the guard in front of him.

As you would expect, his family was outraged. They contacted their congressman, and a full investigation from Washington was imminent. I was still technically the officer in charge and, as they say in the Army, "Shit rolls downhill," meaning that the search for a scapegoat keeps moving down the long chain of command and finally settles on a low-ranking officer or enlisted man.

I deliberately kept a low profile and left the investigation and all follow-up work to others. Luckily, before the blame game really came to a head, I was honorably discharged on June 20, 1968, after having served two years and three months of active duty.

Chapter 29

Civilian Life

*T*hanks to the GI Bill's "no money down" provision, we were able to buy a home in Billerica, a suburb of Boston. It was a twenty-year-old Cape situated on the edge of town, on a small rise above the road that connected Billerica with the towns of Carlisle and Concord. There were two and a half acres of forest behind the house and a farm across the street. We had a small grass yard for the boys to play in.

On a Saturday morning right after we moved in, I was suddenly awakened by the sound of drumbeats. I peered out the second-floor bedroom window and was astounded to see a Fife and Drum Corps from the George Washington era parading by our house. Was I dreaming? Then it dawned on me that they were marching toward Concord as part of the reenactment of the Revolutionary War's Battle of Concord. I had a front-seat viewing of the Billerica Minute Men, who, in 1775, joined up in Concord with militia from other towns to drive the British troops back to Boston.

The Bean Counter

Sandy stayed home with the boys and I went to downtown Boston to join Price Waterhouse. In 1968, personal computers did not exist and large mainframe computers were programmed with a deck of punched cards. The only mechanized tool for audit calculations was the ten-key adding machine.

The first couple of years in large public accounting requires detail checking and verification. All the work was done manually.

Please stay awake for the following example: To verify a billing system, I would select a sample of customer orders and then paw through filing cabinets to pull out each order. I would then go to the shipping dock and paw through another filing cabinet to match each order to its bill of lading. This type of work was tiresome and boring, particularly when I knew that most of the time there was no problem.

I didn't mind doing it because, as in Vietnam, I knew there was an end to it. Also, as promised, I did move from business to business. Surprisingly enough, there was quite a human element involved toward your success in this level of grunt work. For example, your ability to get the full cooperation and respect of the clients' office managers was key, but often difficult, particularly since they knew you had no experience and probably knew very little about how any accounting system worked.

In my case, the gap between the critical nature of my work in the military compared to the work in civilian life was huge. I am sure this is the case with many veterans. It required quite a bit of mental adjustment for me to accept the fact that I, Captain Dobbyn, leader of men, had morphed into Dobbyn the accounting grunt.

During the first year, they assigned me a few small accounts to handle on my own. Eventually I worked on large accounts and supervised others doing the grunt work.

Fun with the "Irish Twins"

Usually, when I came home from work, the boys and I wrestled on the living room shag rug. Since Dylan and Eric were separated by only eleven months, they often enjoyed the same things.

We played tackle football in the side yard. Eric adapted rapidly to the game.

He moved fast and hit hard. When the snow arrived, we rode plastic saucer-shaped sleds from a trail in the woods, through the side yard, and into the fence in front of the house.

We filled up the sunroom with a giant Tinkertoy set that fascinated me. We were able to build a small car with it. In the basement, they raced a tricycle and a Big Wheel around in a figure eight, in and out of the metal support beams.

They had guns that shot Ping-Pong balls, and they ran around the house shooting at each other. Sandy and I took turns reading to them at bedtime. Their favorite was *The Jungle Book*.

I started to teach Dylan how to play chess, and he was very interested. Our kitchen floor was linoleum with red and white squares and, except for the kitchen table and chairs being in the way, would make a nice chessboard. Like the giant Tinkertoys, a chess set with giant plastic pieces was available at a reasonable price. We ordered the set, and the pieces were the perfect size for the "board." What a joy it was to watch Dylan pick up and move the large pieces around.

The Smashed Radio

On the lot next to ours was a ranch-style house with au naturel grounds, inhabited by a man named Sprech Hurd. He was a recently divorced, thirtyish, and new to the area. He had worked with NASA in Cape Canaveral, Florida, and was currently employed by Arthur D. Little, a consulting firm in Boston. He was a technician specializing in the miniaturization of electronics.

On weekends we often chatted while he worked outside on a project or chopped wood. He would occasionally wander over to our house and drop in for a beer. He was a good neighbor.

In the spring of 1969, Sprech invited me over to his house to discuss a business proposition. He had a connection with a psychology graduate student at Harvard named Ralph Schwitz-gebel, who believed that art could be functional. Sprech showed me a prototype of Ralph's creation, which he called the Smashed Radio. It looked like a transistor radio had been lying on a mirror and someone smashed it to pieces it with a hammer. I was somewhat amazed when Sprech clicked the radio on, and it worked. Sprech told me that Ralph had no interest in monetizing the Smashed Radio and that Sprech was free to do so. He had already partnered with a Xerox copier salesman named Todd, and Todd had generated interest from Hammacher Schlemmer, the renowned purveyor of unusual gifts, in New York City. They both believed the Smashed Radio would sell as a decorative conversation piece for a wall or coffee table.

He also showed me another prototype called the Wire Lady, which would be a follow-up project. It was a wire sculpture of a woman kneeling on both knees with a high-end FM radio wired inside. She was holding what looked like a bowl but was the radio's speaker, and the on/off and volume controls were on her chest.

My entrepreneurial juices started flowing. I told Sprech I was very interested.

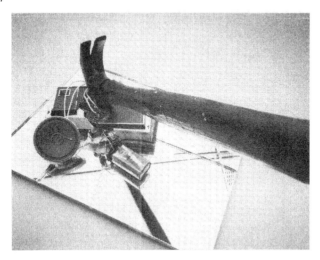

Smashed radio

I didn't take to Todd at our first meeting. He was fast-talking and a little too sure of himself. On the other hand, he had opened the door to the best possible and maybe the only customer, Hammacher Schlemmer. I agreed to join them. We funded the venture equally and agreed to do so going forward.

Sprech found a small ramshackle shop on a side street off Central Square in Cambridge, which we leased for practically nothing. You get what you pay for. We spent a few weekends just making it slightly habitable.

Todd went off to New York to meet with Hammacher Schlemmer and returned with a test order for several radios and the promise that, if we performed successfully in filling that order, many more would follow.

I arranged for the purchase of radios, mirrors, hammers, backing, and epoxy. Since we all had full-time jobs, we hired a Harvard student to help us part-time with production.

The orders started flowing in when we got in the catalog. It was clear to me that we needed to risk building a lot of inventory to meet the likely Christmas increase in orders. I explained to my partners that we needed to put more cash in the business and increase the production significantly. But they were reluctant to take the risk.

Life magazine did an article on unusual Christmas gifts. One entire page was dedicated to a picture of the Smashed Radio. We were ecstatic! Shortly after that, *The Tonight Show*, hosted by Johnny Carson, did a segment on unusual Christmas gifts and featured the Smashed Radio. The orders rolled in!

It has been said that the only thing in business worse than too little business is too much business. We worked late nights and long weekends. My brother Denny was available and came up from Providence to help out. In spite of our efforts, we didn't come close to building enough units to meet the order demand. Hammacher Schlemmer deemed us an unreliable supplier and canceled our orders. Since that company was the only one known to us to be interested in our unique product, and because we did not have the capital to market the radio directly to individuals, we were forced to close up shop.

The lessons I learned were to be extremely careful with whom you go into business and to make sure you have enough cash to finance the start-up. Years later, I had apparently forgotten these lessons, because I bought into a business in Florida with two people I hardly knew. Suffice it to say it also did not end well.

Terribly Sorry, Mr. Renzi

The personnel manager at PW was Dick Kendrick. He was a personable soul and handled the staff assignments. I think he respected the fact that I was a veteran and older than most of my junior peers. He assigned me to some high-profile clients and a good mix of small and large jobs.

One day he stopped me in the hallway and asked how things were going. We chatted a little and then he said that he heard I played the drums. I confirmed the rumor.

Every year, after tax season, Price Waterhouse had a dinner dance for all their employees and their spouses. Dick was trying to put together some of the musical talent in the office to play a few tunes when the orchestra took a break. He had commitments from Harold, an audit senior who played bass guitar, Tom, from the copy room who played lead guitar, and Richard, also from the copy room, who was a singer.

The event was only two weeks away. We met briefly in the office and agreed that we could learn two songs in one practice session. We rehearsed in the basement of my house. After a couple of hours, we had "Jeremiah Was a Bullfrog" and "Proud Mary" by Creedence Clearwater Revival sounding pretty respectable.

The dinner dance was held in the main ballroom of the Statler Hotel in Boston. In 1969 the bands at this type of event played light jazz and pop standards, but very little, if any, rock 'n' roll. When we launched into "Jeremiah," it was like a musical dam breaking as everyone took to the dance floor. We received a huge round of applause. After we played "Proud Mary," the applause was even louder. It wasn't us; it was the times. Rock 'n' roll was finding its way into all aspects of society.

Maybe it was partly us, because later that evening Tom was approached by someone who was planning a party on a Boston Harbor Cruise boat. We were riding high and took the gig.

We held a couple of practice sessions at my home and added four more songs to our repertoire. When we played aboard the boat, I don't think anybody noticed that we played the same songs at least twice. Maybe it was because the seas had picked up a little. I had a difficult time playing, because my bass drum kept sliding across the deck away from me.

A week or so later, Tom called and said that he and Richard wondered if I would be interested in continuing to play with them. Harold wasn't interested, but Tom recruited another excellent bass player to replace him.

I said I would play if we played only a night or two on weekends. We started practicing one night a week and broadened our repertoire. Tom was our leader and Richard had a beautifully smooth voice, which shined when he soloed on a slow love song. We got a couple of one-night gigs, one at the Dorchester Yacht Club and one at a dive in Nantasket Beach. Accountant by day, rock star by night!

A month or so later, Tom told me that Dick Kendrick had asked him if we would be interested in doing a wedding. He said an Italian relative was looking for a band, and he'd recommended us. He suggested that if we learned a couple of Italian songs, including the "Tarantella," and Richard sang a Sinatra song or two, we could pull it off. Tom always did the announcements and song introductions, but he was not comfortable with the narration duties of a wedding. I had done a lot of public speaking in the Army and gladly volunteered to be the MC.

The wedding reception was held at the Chateau de Ville in Framingham. It was a popular venue for functions and also for visiting musical entertainers. The groom was a son of the Renzi family from New York and the bride was a Panicucci from the Boston area.

The room filled up rapidly and the guests seemed to enjoy our music, particularly the young ladies. Richard was hitting on all cylinders. I had handled the preliminary announcements and was ready for the grand entrance of the bride and groom.

All the overhead lights in the room were shut off, leaving only the glow of candles on the tables. A spotlight then lit up the entrance to the room.

With great joy in my voice, I announced, "Ladies and gentlemen! For the first time as man and wife...Mr. and Mrs. Panicucci!" There was a horrible silence. What was wrong?

Behind me, Tom whispered loudly, "That's the bride's name."

I felt sick inside as I blurted out, "I'm sorry, I meant to say... actually they are Mr. and Mrs. Renzi."

It was then that everyone applauded.

For the rest of the evening, as couples danced by the stage, I got some looks that could kill. Some of the men looked like they were quite capable of doing just that.

I felt like such a jerk. I couldn't get the blunder out of my mind. I had trouble sleeping the next few nights.

Cruising the Concord River

Taking advantage of the fact that the Concord River flows right through Billerica, Sandy and I bought a sturdy Grumman aluminum canoe. With its small electric motor, the four of us did indeed cruise. We would bring food, drinks, a blanket, and the Sunday paper to picnic on the shore.

I bought two small fishing poles to amuse the boys while we relaxed back from the shore on the blanket. I figured that even though they wouldn't catch anything, it would keep them busy for an hour or so. Much to our amazement, Eric was back in about fifteen minutes with a good-size pickerel flopping around on his line. The pickerel was just the beginning. In later years, fish feared him whenever he picked up a pole.

Chapter 30

A Shocking Development

When you sign up with the Army, it's a seven-year commitment. After your active-duty tour, you become a member of the inactive reserve. Usually you stay inactive. However, they can call you back to active duty anytime.

Two years after my active-duty tour ended, I received orders in the mail stating I was to report in July to Camp Pickett, Virginia, for two weeks of active duty. I was assigned to a National Guard Military Police battalion out of Pittsburgh, which was there for their annual training.

I was astounded and incredibly angry. I could just imagine some overly zealous staff officer at the Pentagon coming up with the brilliant idea that returning vets could be used to train National Guard units.

At that time, National Guard and Reserve units were rarely activated. In fact, those wishing to stay out of the war flocked into the National Guard and Reserve units. Political influence was often required to get in. So my life was being interrupted to train those who would never see active duty. Good thing I had not thrown out my uniforms, including jungle fatigues.

An Unwelcome Welcome

Dressed in civilian clothes, I flew to Richmond and then took a bus to Blackstone some fifty miles farther inland. Another bus transported me and some of the other reservists to the base. On the way to Camp Pickett, I overheard some fellas complaining loudly about being called up. After check-in, I was directed to the headquarters building.

Outside the building I ran into a Major Brown and introduced myself. He was the battalion executive officer (XO, second-in-command). "You will be taking my job, Captain," he announced with a smile on his face.

"The hell I will, Major. You need the training, and I am done with the Army," I retorted.

We went inside together to see the CO, Colonel Bilby. Brown immediately reported my insubordination. I made my case about training and added that I was not very pleased to be there.

The colonel told me that a first lieutenant and twelve enlisted men had also been called to duty, and he was not sure how to deploy them. I recommended that he put me in charge of these men and use us as the aggressor force, playing the role of the bad guys during maneuvers. He liked the idea. The XO was really pissed to get his job back.

The Aggressive "Aggressor Force"

I met with my new aggressor force before the colonel could change his mind. Most of the men had been in Vietnam. They were absolutely enraged at having their civilian lives disrupted.

I explained our mission and suggested that we could really

work off our anger by being the best aggressor force we could be. One of the men came up to me after the meeting, and it turned out he had been in my platoon in Saigon. During the Tet Offensive, he was in one of the Alert Force trucks that were ambushed in the same alley I had warned my successor about. He told me that when they were attacked, he was able to get out of the truck and jump into the doorway of one of the buildings that lined the alleyway. He tried to return fire, but the hail of bullets kept him pinned down. He showed me the bullet scars he had on his hand and wrist.

The fact that the Army called up a soldier who had earned a Purple Heart and most likely was working through some level of PTSD, to play games with a reserve unit, made me furious. I decided to motivate and develop scenarios for my aggressor force to be as disruptive as possible. Game on!

The first training scenario was the convoy escort. I had placed my men along the route to fire blanks and throw smoke grenades at the convoy. Part of the convoy escort mission was the operation of traffic control posts (TCP). Basically, they just directed traffic at intersections.

I went ahead of the convoy to the TCP. I told the two soldiers manning the post that they were officially dead. I told them to take off their shirts and give them to my men. My men, now disguised as guards, diverted the convoy of a jeep and two trucks to the left, down a hill.

I did not realize that the bottom of the hill was very wet and muddy with red clay. What a bonus! The trucks became mired in the red clay, clogging up everything.

That night at the officers' club, the XO came up and sat next to me at the bar. He was really pissed that he had spent the greater part of the day trying to extricate the two trucks. I told him it was good training. He told me to go fuck myself.

What a Riot!

At that time, Camp Pickett was used only for reserve unit training. There were many vacant barracks throughout. The XO had picked out a street with several of these abandoned barracks as the site for the riot-control scenario.

I deployed my force inside the barrack at the end of the street and gave orders to start making a lot of noise in the building when the troops arrived. At my signal, they were to run out into the street to confront them, as rioters would.

The XO, his staff, and a platoon of about sixty MPs arrived in trucks at the head of the street. While they were forming up, the aggressor force started smashing windows and yelling insults at the MPs.

I think the Army manual on riot control had not been updated since World War I. As per the manual, they lined up shoulder to shoulder across the street. They held their rifles out waist high with bayonets attached. In unison, they moved forward one step at a time.

Meanwhile, the "rioters" had gone into a raucous frenzy. Sinks, toilets, and bedspring pieces, never to be used, were flying out the windows. They were enjoying themselves, and so was I. They were really pumped up when they ran out into the street. They charged the first line of MPs and then jumped back while laughing and screaming. The MPs slowed down. The aggressors kept up the mock attacks. I pulled my guys back before anyone got hurt.

Night Ninjas

We worked up a plan of attack for when the whole battalion went on bivouac (camping out). The training scenario was perimeter defense and security. My plan was to have us move in around midnight, fire a few blanks at the guards, and then retire.

My boys infiltrated the perimeter, which was not difficult since most of the guards were asleep. They surrounded the colonel's tent and woke up everyone. They laughed their asses off as the CO called an end to the exercise. I had now earned the wrath of both the CO and the XO.

You Cannot Be Serious

The XO personally involved himself in the VIP escort exercise. He replicated a contingent of visiting dignitaries from the Middle East. Three of his dark-complexioned men wore Arabian-type headdresses. They were passengers in his Cadillac convertible as they drove all around the camp. MPs, armed with rifles, darted their jeeps ahead and behind the Caddy to provide protection.

I had two more days and a wake-up before my release. As usual, I was at the officers' club bar stuck in the company of my nemesis. He was in a good mood and proud of the first VIP escort mission he put on. I told him that it was really innovative and impressive.

As part of my disruptive plan, I suggested that it would be great for community relations if he ran the exercise through town as a demonstration for the good citizens of Blackstone. He thought it was a terrific idea, particularly after I volunteered to do the work and make the arrangements with the town. The following night,

I told him that arrangements had been made for the mayor to greet him the next day at the steps of City Hall at 1400 hours. Of course, I had done nothing of the sort.

On the big day, I grabbed a couple of beers and drove off into the woods to do some four-wheeling and to wait for all hell to break loose. I returned to headquarters in the late afternoon and was met by the battalion clerk. "Sir, the colonel wants to see you—he is really upset."

I was filled with apprehension about what I had done when I entered the CO's office. "Captain!" he ranted. "I received a call from the mayor of Blackstone. He was very upset about having the major pull up to his front door, with some Arabs in his car, asking to see him. Also, his office has been inundated with calls from folks in town wondering who the grand pooh-bah was in the Cadillac, escorted by the Military Police, riding through their town."

"What does this have to do with me, sir? It's the major's operation," I said.

"Major Brown here says that you set all this up with the mayor's office," he retorted.

I feigned shock: "First of all, I never thought he would take me seriously, and second, it is against Army regulations to conduct military training exercises off base! What the hell were you thinking, Brown?"

They just looked at each other. Then the CO said: "You are dismissed, Captain."

I turned on my heel, without saluting, and marched out of the colonel's office and permanently back into civilian life.

Shortly after my return home from Camp Pickett, I celebrated my twenty-seventh birthday. Scientists say that the male brain is physically developed by the age of twenty-seven but full emotional development is not reached until age forty-two. It has been three decades and then some past my forty-second birthday, and my complete maturity appears to be unattainable.

Acknowledgments

Special thanks to Betsy Thorpe and her literary services team. Betsy is easy to work with and her editorial suggestions were insightful and key to bringing the book together. Penina Lopez's copyediting left no stone unturned.

If my mother and father and my uncle Jack were here, I would thank them for the letters they left behind, some of which are included in this memoir. My stepfather, Joe Collins, dug out the papers documenting my father's service in the Army, which were critical to the telling of his story.

I am extremely grateful for the contributions of the following family members:

My sister Bobbie suffered through a review of my first rough draft, which showed me that I had a long way to go.

My brother Mark, author of *The Heartspace Portal*, shared his book-creation experience and offered suggestions on how to develop writing work habits.

My sister Chrissy was my historian. I called on her countless times to fill in the blanks in my memory as to the what, when, where, and why of family situations and relationships. My brother Denny, my sister Phyllis, and my son Dylan also assisted in this recollection and verification process.

My wife, Dee, convinced me that my efforts to tell my stories were worthwhile, and she was an invaluable sounding board all along the way.

About the Author

Dick, aka Rick, grew up in Boston and Providence. He was educated by the Saint Joseph nuns, the Christian brothers, and the Jesuit priests. He graduated from Boston College with a BS in accounting. He was in the ROTC program at BC and received a commission as an Army officer in the Military Police. He served in Vietnam and stateside and escaped with an honorable discharge. Despite a weakness in mathematics, Dick earned a CPA while working for Price Waterhouse (PWC) in Boston. The stories in his memoir are from this rowdy and chaotic period in his life.

The academic knowledge from BC, the leadership experience from the Army, and the hands-on accounting skills at PWC all contributed to a thirty-five-year career in financial management. Along the way, he was a drummer and a video gamer and he loved to mess around with boats. He worked for several international manufacturing companies and retired as the chief financial officer of a manufacturer in Sarasota, Florida. Dick and his wife, Dee, currently live in Fort Mill, South Carolina.

Made in the USA
Middletown, DE
11 September 2021